MW01295156

i

Copyright © 2018 by Colin Molaski

All rights reserved. No part of this publication may be reproduced, distributed, or transmitted in any form or by any means, including photocopying, recording, or other electronic or mechanical methods, without the prior written permission of the publisher, except in the case of brief quotations embodied in critical reviews and certain other noncommercial uses permitted by copyright law.

Printed in the United States of America

First Printing, 2018

ISBN: 978-1729839324

CreateSpace Publishing, LLC
7281 Investment Drive
N. Charleston, SC 29418
A subsidiary of Amazon, Inc.

GROWING UP

on

ADDERALL:

an introspective memoir

COLIN MOLASKI

For my gentle, beautiful, intelligent
soul of a daughter:
my life, my breath, my everything.

I love you, sweetheart.

➤ ACKNOWLEDGEMENTS

I would first like to thank my longtime friend and barber, Mr. Bernard Franklin, for showing me the importance of reading and learning. His inspiration is what first sparked my thirst for the truth and fueled my drive to continually read, study, think, and finally pass on my experience to others. I am forever grateful for his sage advice and guidance.

I would also like to thank my editor, Mr. Steven Conifer, for his thorough and tireless work on the original manuscript of this book. Without him, this final version would doubtless be infinitely inferior to what, I am sure, I likely would have produced on my own.

And, of course, I am endlessly indebted to mother and father, not only for their incredible patience, love, and attentiveness in parenting me (no easy task, to say the least), but also for lending me their laptop; without it, writing this book would have been a logistical nightmare, tedious in the extreme.

Finally, I would be remiss if I didn't acknowledge my sweet and beautiful daughter, Stella. She has been an inextinguishable light and inexhaustible source of strength, even – perhaps especially – in the darkest, bleakest moments of my life. My darling girl, though you probably can't understand this now, I know that someday you will: you, more than anyone or anything else, afford me the courage and resolve to tackle life's seemingly countless adversities, to press on and give it my all no matter what. To provide for you the best life possible is the most important role I'll ever play. *Daddy loves you forever and always.*

Growing Up
on
Adderall

➤ CHAPTER 1

I write this, not because I claim to have any real answers, but because of the experiences that have inspired me to find such answers, to seek the truth no matter how elusive it might seem. The truth is funny like that: try as we might to avoid it, it always has a way of sneaking up behind us, sooner or later, and reminding us just how fragile and powerless we really are, that whatever control we think we have over our own lives and destinies is ultimately illusory. Truth is maybe the most powerful weapon one can have in his arsenal. It is the great equalizer of men, as it were, great and small. It is "anti-fragile," almost impervious, a personal kryptonite of sorts: the more one tries to duck, dodge, damage, or conceal it, the bigger and stronger, the more visible and dominant it becomes. And as for that old failsafe, the passage of time? No, as the passing of months and years do not weaken, but in fact only *bolster* it. It is truly a force to be reckoned with, this almighty Truth.

My journey hasn't exactly followed a clear line across a well-drawn map; if anything, quite the opposite is true: it has been, in large measure, a journey through chaos, creating order out of disorder, salvaging identity from the ashes of obscurity, converting flaws into assets and defeat into strength. I hold no special powers, know of no shortcuts, and possess absolutely no secret knowledge whatsoever. To be sure, all I have – indeed, all *any* of us have - is "the now," and, with a little luck and practice, the ability to communicate with each other clearly and effectively (and, in my case, to quench my thirst for creative expression).

In order for me to properly relate just how I got to where I am, I will need, of course, to start at the very beginning. The very beginning, for me, also happens to provide the setting of my first-ever memory, which has the added benefit of being the most logical place to start. (In truth, whether this memory is my actual first or not isn't entirely clear to me; but, given the clarity and significance of the memory itself, for my purposes here I'll simply proceed as if it were.)

With all that prefatory business now out of the way, let me take you back to when...

I was lying on my back in my crib. It was slated, with spaces in between the framing so I was able to see through it. I remember there was a mobile hanging above me. I can still see it clearly if I close my eyes and let my mind wander back there. The important part, why I remember it so well, is not the baby mobile itself, however; it's that I turned over on my side, toward the wall, and suddenly saw something very odd and out of place. Even to my infant mind, it felt like a very dark and malevolent energy, alarmingly near me, hovering just beside me.

From what I've learned over the years, children are extremely susceptible to seeing and feeling energies largely unnoticed by adults, mostly because of the programming to which we're all subjected as we get older: we're trained by the mundanities of daily life, as it were, simply to look past such things, to see only surfaces and miss altogether that which lurks beneath them. Now that I reflect on the bizarre occasion, it makes a bit more sense to me.

For some reason I want to say that this shape (as we'll call it for the sake of simplicity) was vaguely snake-like in form. I recall being aware of its presence in my room and my taking an immediate dislike to it. Of course, I couldn't understand any of that at the time, but could only feel the fright and confusion any infant (or child) would at such a sight. To this day I have no idea what the thing was, what of significance (if anything) its presence represented, or its purpose in "visiting" me. All I know is that it tried to get close to me, but for some peculiar reason it never could, or perhaps just didn't want to.

2

Even though I come from a wonderful and loving family, as a kid I never felt quite a part of it, oddly enough. It seemed, all throughout my childhood, as if there were some inexplicable barrier between me and my parents, and (though to a somewhat lesser extent) my sister. Perhaps the root cause of this disconnect was my inability to be honest with them, or with myself – which, in turn, was probably the result of some fear I had that, if I *were* more open with them, they might reject me somehow, dismiss my feelings as silly, mostly as "adolescent angst." I used to think I always felt different from the rest of the world, but now I wonder just how common that feeling actually is, especially among children and teenagers. I constantly felt isolated, as I suppose many if not most teenagers do, and seemingly unable to overcome the feeling. This feeling would persist well into my early adulthood, and even to this day haunts me at times. But back then, unlike now, everything was so black and white.

I grew up at the end of a little cul-de-sac in a big college town called Bellingham, Washington. The name of the street I lived on was Likely Court. To this day I still remember the address: 2614 Likely Court. Ours was a decently sized, well-kept two-story house, in which my mother and father raised my sister and me. Even as kids go, I was exceedingly energetic; I just never stopped doing, talking, thinking – the works. I was also deeply curious, an inquisitive child who no doubt drove the adults around me nuts with my endless (and to them naturally quite silly) questions, including the time-honored infinite regress of "Whys?" for which young children are world-famous.

I wanted to try anything and everything, mess with anything I could possibly get my hands on. The world was my playground. Even at a very young age I relished being and playing outside. I mean, I lived for it. God, it always felt so good to be outside! That most of us, as we approach adulthood, quickly become accustomed to spending at least half our waking lives indoors, mostly confined to cubicles, still strikes me as something of a tragedy. To be able to run out that door and have the fresh air rush against my face and soak into my pores… ah, no feeling could compare to it, let me tell you.

I detested being still, sitting inside, waiting for something exciting to happen – waiting on some action. Already, it seems, I had begun to realize that life is lived on the wire.

➢ CHAPTER 2

I was bursting with so much energy, in fact, that even in my earliest formative years I quickly found myself getting into all sorts of trouble.

Pre-school, I've always thought, is a very strange environment. Mine, perhaps, was *particularly* strange. Looking back now, I wonder if my classmates share my vivid and (in some cases, anyway) rather intense memories of the place. Even as I sit here now, with my eyes closed, I can smell the bleach and cleaning supplies with every deep breath I take. It's like I'm standing in the hallway again, about to get dropped off by my mother for the day. I can still make out the bright, cheap fluorescent lights in the kitchen and hallway. I can still feel the moist soil squishing through my fingers as I dig for worms – and remember, this is going back a good twenty years, as of this writing: so vivid, so strong, are my memories of the time and place. So real and, well… *immediate.* (The place at which I attended pre-school is now an abandoned building, all boarded up and vandalized. It saddens me to see it like that, as my memories of it are every bit as fond as they are clear.)

Back then, when I was all of four or five years old, even a *fence* couldn't contain my energy! It's funny – and more than a little bittersweet, if I'm to be frank about it – to look back now and realize that, even from my first days as an upright, semi-self-aware human being, my behaviors were those of somebody who showed complete disregard to any forms of self-control and moderation. Already, at such a tender age (I was, after all, barely old enough to use the bathroom on my own), I seemed almost helplessly drawn to any and all forms of escapism.

The story I'll now relate takes place on the playground during recess, on a particularly gorgeous, sunny day. All around me I felt warmth and energy. An older kid, whose name I remember was Max, pointed to the old, weathered wooden fence that tracked the perimeter of the backyard playground. He and I then darted over to a certain spot at the base of the fence, at which, at some point, he must have spied a small hole dug out underneath it (as if by a dog hunting for its previously buried bone). For some reason my first impulse was to shimmy through that tiny tunnel, to escape - though there was absolutely nothing, mind you, at least so far as I can remember, from which I felt any particular need (or even desire) *to* escape: I just wanted to, I think, because I *could.*

So there I was, trying to make the hole a bit wider so as to facilitate my spontaneous self-liberation from the oppressive chains of mandatory pre-K. The principal promptly spotted me, figured out what I was up to, and came galloping down off the porch, yelling my name and demanding that I "cut it out, Colin, cut that nonsense *out* right this very instant!" (or words to that effect). I was, of course, captured well before I could wiggle my way to freedom. I wasn't sent home – not that day, anyway – but the principal did, in due course, rat me out to my parents. I ought to ask my parents some time if they remember the incident; and, if so, whether it marked the first occasion on which they began to suspect their son might have issues with "impulse control." I imagine, whether they remember the saga of the "attempted playground escape" or not, they would say they had their suspicions regarding my congenital impulsivity long before it ever took place.

The takeaway here, is that, for as far back as I can remember, family, friends, teachers, even society at large has tried their absolute hardest, usually with the best of intentions, to keep me from being the person I was meant to be. That sort of organized, structured, constant suppression, in turn, led me to violate wherever I could the restrictions and limitations that are imposed upon all of us from young. I'm not blaming the principal for stopping me, though: in fact, I'm quite thankful that she did. Rather, I merely wonder sometimes: what about the environment of the place made me want me to escape it so badly? Or did it have little or nothing to do with the environment, as I've sort of already suggested, and everything (or almost everything) to do with me? That's the question – symbolically speaking, as applied to innumerable places on countless occasions across a two-decade span – to which I've long sought an answer.

It wasn't long after that episode occurred that a certain behavioral pattern emerged: more and more outbursts over time, with shorter and shorter intervals in between, both on the playground and elsewhere. At this point it must have just been about attention, because I had no concept of obeying authority figures beyond simply heeding (or not) the cries of my teachers and principals to "Come inside!" at the end of recess each day – and, therefore, no real sense of what rebellion would even look like, much less an inclination toward it.

I had a favorite tree out on that playground. It sat in the same general vicinity as the hole through which I'd endeavored, albeit somewhat half-heartedly, to stage a spectacular escape scene. This tree wasn't just any old, ordinary tree: no, this thing had *character* (to me, anyway). If I pause and clear my mind and picture it from ground to crown, I can almost feel the deep, rough grooves in the bark of its trunk, zig-zagging ruts winding through the dense wood, big enough that I could run my four-year-old fingers through them. And, very often, I did just that, savoring the texture of the bark but also sizing up the tree itself for a potential climb. Each limb had a familiar, worn-out smoothness to it. It was extremely inviting. I spent as much time in that tree as the staff would let me, my legs crossed on the branches and head resting on the back on a limb.

Maybe it sounds a bit silly now, but when I was in that tree, I would always pretend to be my favorite gargoyle from the popular '90s cartoon *Gargoyles*. One day I was perched in my "gargoyle" tree, just scanning the playground for something interesting, anything upon which to fix my ever-hungry attention. It was as if I were subconsciously wired to place myself into situations, whenever possible, in which making impulsive (and usually ill-advised)

7

decisions would be particularly easy. Sure enough, one did: suddenly there appeared in my line of sight a perfectly inflated beach ball, presumably left behind by some other boys who'd since lost interest in it. The especially vivid part of this memory is my immediately scooting out of the tree and toward this enchanting object I'd spotted, this ball, as if drawn to it by some magnetic force beyond my power to resist. I moved almost robotically, with terrific purpose and breakneck speed, having resolved in an instant that I would reach the ball, grab the ball, and sprint off with it to some place more to my liking... say, perhaps my "gargoyle" tree?

On my way back to the tree, ball now securely in my possession (and, near as I could tell, my spontaneous appropriation of it thus far undetected), I paused briefly to snatch up a sliver of bark lying on the playground floor. This detour completed, I then carted my pair of treasures up into my secret spot within the "gargoyle" tree. And then, so suddenly and "out of nowhere" that anyone watching would doubtless have been quite taken aback, I took the sharp chunk of bark and stabbed its point into the beach ball, then smiled with a rather perverse, distinctly juvenile satisfaction as I watched the colorful toy rapidly deflate in my lap, withering eventually into a flaccid, formless lump of plastic. Once the deflation was complete, I simply tossed the ball aside and went about my business (whatever that might have been back then, most likely an afternoon nap).

Rather odd, wouldn't you say? Or maybe not. Maybe little boys are just inherently destructive creatures. In any event, there's certainly plenty of evidence for the proposition – and I, for one, was no exception to it.

That's hardly the only example from my youth of an incident arising, it seems to me in hindsight, entirely from excess energy. I lacked even a rough idea of "healthy outlets" for this hyperactivity, and was therefore doomed, I must suppose now, to channel it through... shall we say, "alternate means" (particularly damaging school property, another favorite childhood activity of mine)?

Fortunately, piercing the beach ball with the splinter of bark that day *had* seemed to curb this appetite for destruction, at least in large measure, for in the weeks and months that followed, I actually found myself in trouble at school significantly less often than I had previously.

Which leads me to wonder: is allowing children to manifest their manic energy in such ways (i.e., by means of relatively harmless if less-than-ideal, "non-constructive" behaviors) perhaps well-advised, if only in the long run? In other words, is allowing them to "be themselves," even if it means letting them act out a bit wildly or feverishly at times, perhaps not ultimately preferable to trying (in most cases fruitlessly, of course) to hinder such expression? I, at any rate, have begun to think it just might be, both from a disciplinary standpoint and one which seeks to foster children's emotional growth, to let them learn from their mistakes and thereby mature faster and more fully, more naturally, than is perhaps achieved through so-called "helicopter parenting" (and "helicoptering" by the other adults in their lives, such as their aunts, uncles, teachers, coaches, and so on).

Maybe this explains why, even way back then (at the tender age of five or six), I intuitively understood how best to manage my own stormy impulses, at least in many cases. Which perhaps implies that it's the same way for other kids, for children generally: maybe, just maybe, we'd be better off as a society if we simply permitted our little ones to act on at least *some* of their scarier urges, despite the apparent irresponsibility of doing so. That is, frightening as the prospect might seem at first thought, and even if their doing so might involve some superficially "bad" behaviors in the moment, to let our young ones scratch some of their more innocuous if juvenile itches might well prove advantageous to young and old alike. It might do this, essentially, by enabling the kids to purge much of their nervous energy (without causing anyone irreparable harm, of course), thereby curbing far more pernicious conduct later in life. And this, in turn, would be good for the grown-ups in that, first of all, it would save them a whole lot of grief filled face to face child-rearing; secondly, it would stamp out, and choke off before they had a chance to really take root and do some lasting psychological damage, a great many otherwise inevitable resentments on the part of the kids toward their elders; and finally, it would just make for a healthier, happier, more functional society overall. Or so the theory goes, anyway.

The productivity was always there; just the structure was lacking. Again, the beach ball incident was a perfect illustration: I poured into its destruction precisely the energy and focus that I could have used, instead, to play with it as it had been designed to be played with, like a "normal" kid. But I *didn't* simply play with it; I decimated the thing, as completely and efficiently as a professional beach-ball hitman. (Come to think of it, that may have been my very first act of *self*-destruction, so to speak, in a totally childlike and unconscious fashion: the ball was me; the shard of bark was my weapon; the act was self-punishment of a sort, presumably for some perceived blunder or shortcoming such as only a four-year-old could blame himself for.)

Throughout pre-school, most of my (especially) troubling or dramatic behavior unfolded on the playground. Like I said before, there was something about being outside and inhaling that fresh air straight into my lungs, something about the way my pores soaked up all that beautiful, invigorating sunshine, that always seemed to infuse my body with uncontrollable energy. The next episode I'm going to tell you about was very much a case in point.

The jungle gym at my pre-school was made partly of wood and partly of steel, was located right smack in the middle of the playground. To me it felt old and weathered, with a bit of character about it. I loved to climb on everything I could on that playground (or try to, at least), whether it was technically off-limits or not. On this particular occasion, prior to my positioning myself just so on the jungle gym, I had gone over to the pile of dirt on the outskirts of the fence and dug out a small handful of fresh worms, these now writhing stupidly on my slick, soil-stained palm. Finally, all set for the main event, presently I climbed one side of the jungle gym and positioned myself atop the bar that kids typically used to slide themselves down to the ground – more *typical* kids, that is. From my privileged vantage point, I had a bird's-eye view of anyone who might be brave (or foolish) enough to approach. Ha-ha! I was, in that moment, reigning king of my post-toddler domain.

Soon, I spied some poor, innocent girl making her way toward the jungle gym. I readied my nerves, my feet, my hands. (*A girl*, I thought giddily, deviously. *How perfect!*) Just as she began to sprint under the bars, which is to say, underneath *me*, I extended my arm so that my hand was right above her head and opened my fist and allowed the small handful of dirty worms I'd previously collected to fall directly onto the helpless little girl's head. exactly as I'd hoped for, she pealed a series of shocked, terrified screams, which in turn attracted the playground chaperone's attention once again.

Up to this point, I still had not been diagnosed with ADHD or any other alphabet-disorder such as shrinks and counselors nowadays seem to attach to kids as blithely as coaches hand out participation awards. (I hadn't yet so much as seen a doctor, in fact.) Now, don't get me wrong: kids will be kids, as well they should be, but even by less modern, knee-jerk, "Oh, my goodness, Billy threw a rock, he must be a murderer-in-the-making" standards, my behavior deviated considerably, I'm told, from that of the larger class; I stood out from the crowd, in other words, and not usually for the better. As far as I know, none of my classmates *ever* dropped live, filthy worms on anyone during my pre-school days. Even then, apparently, my desire for attention, to be different in some substantial way from my peers and thereby establish myself clearly as a rebel, a nonconformist, a troublemaker, was unmistakable. Whatever my urge in a given moment, more often than not I would act on it, without any regard whatsoever for the likely consequences (for myself *or* others, I might add). That character trait would eventually take the form less of outright defiance and more commonly of endless self-questioning and self-doubt, a personality quirk most of the adults in my life would come to see as simple, quintessentially adolescent stubbornness.

"You're argumentative, Colin" (and similar statements) would become a constant refrain first as I approached, and later all throughout, my high school years.

But long before any of *that* took place, I quickly learned how to transform my energetic impulses into cunning manipulations wherever possible. In pre-school (without medication, remember), we were frequently scheduled a nap-time period where most of the kids would be required to roll out their blankets or towels, take out a book (or not), and then try to nap for about forty-five minutes. To me, this was, without a doubt, the very worst part of the school day; I feared it, even, *dreaded* it, because – yep, you guessed it – I was required to actually *sit still!* (Well, *lie* still, actually, but you get my point). For an extended period, no less! I positively loathed even slowing down; actually *resting*, being calm and quiet for more than two minutes at a stretch, was virtually beyond my capabilities back then. (To a lesser degree, I'll confess, it still is.)

When a child as energetic as I is deprived, even for a short while, of all the usual stimuli (toys, games, art, even simple social interaction), the results aren't likely to be happy ones. Trying to get me to actually *sleep* was like trying to get directions from a newborn baby: flat-out impossible. Just wasn't going to happen. So yeah, it didn't take me long to develop an almost bodily, automatic aversion to "nap time." As that terrifying forty-five-minute block of time drew closer, I'd often break out in a cold sweat, nervously pacing the length of the room, debating whether to make a break for it (okay, so maybe I'm exaggerating a *little* bit, but not much, I swear). During these designated downtimes, certain children, whose parents had paid a special fee in advance, were able to skip their naps altogether and go outside, where the gym bus was parked, and play inside it.

Lest you aren't familiar with so-called "gym buses," let me explain. To kids around my age at the time, being granted access to the gym bus was a big deal, and actually playing inside it probably one of the coolest experiences you could ever hope to have. Alas, little Colin would never himself be given that chance, because that "special fee" was too steep for his parents to afford (or, at any rate, steeper than they were willing to pay). Even today, I can clearly picture the bus: it was a charming, somewhat antiquated affair, average in length, painted off-white with baby blue trim around the top edges of the roof. Upon entry, the lucky tyke was immediately greeted by an indoor ball pit. The whole floor was carpeted with some sort of dark, grayish withered fabric (Berber carpet, if I were to guess now). The inside seemed to expand more and more the farther you went back. To a child, the attractions (obstacles, really) must have seemed countless. There was a set of monkey bars, a rolling mat, a wedged mat one could run up, and all sorts of toys to complete the experience. It truly was mind blowing back then.

While I never officially made the gym bus "list," I did decide one day that, somehow, I was nevertheless entitled to explore it. (In this way, my penetration of this off-limits, almost mythical territory was perhaps an early example of my impulse-control issues taking the form of manipulation, of "working the system.") There was a child whom, I had carefully noted, would go to the gym bus every Friday during nap time. Well, one Friday he must have been sick, or was absent for some other reason. In any case, before nap time came around that day, I decided that I was going to escape the dull requirements of "downtime" and get on that blasted gym bus, once and for all.

I waited as patiently as I could (which, for me, wasn't very patiently at all) for the other kids to go outside and get in line. It was at that moment that I told the teacher I needed to go to the bathroom, and when I got up, I walked outside to the playground, toward the line of kids at the back of the bus. When I got there, I just sort of blended myself into the group, and when the chaperone went down the list of names of those eligible for admittance, I said "here" when she called out the name of the boy who was absent that day. To my sheer amazement and utter delight, it actually worked! I was granted access to the bus, if only for ten fleeting minutes, until the teacher noticed I'd never returned from the "bathroom" and came looking for me.

Sure enough, there I was, happy as could be, attacking all the varied and wondrous obstacles inside the hallowed gym bus. She was... well, annoyed, sure, but I think also maybe a little bit impressed.

In the beginning I never went looking for trouble; I only went looking for an outlet for my wild impulses because, without one, sooner or later I typically found myself in trouble regardless. (Interestingly, it was nearly always adults and adults alone who seemed to look unfavorably upon my behavior in such situations, never my friends or other children generally.) Flash forward a year to kindergarten. The environment was completely different from that of pre-school, but my behavior hadn't changed a bit. Evidently my surroundings had little or nothing to do with my energy levels.

My kindergarten teacher's name was Mrs. Sponick. (Don't ask me how I still remember her name; I still surprise myself at times.) She was an amiable woman and a conscientious teacher. I've always thought highly of her. At any rate, around halfway through my kindergarten school year , Mrs. Sponick announced that she would be absent for the rest of the school year on account of her being pregnant, and that she would be replaced by a younger, "greener" teacher. I'll admit it: I don't even remember the replacement teacher's name. I'm not sure why, really, especially since (at least in my eyes) she was far less superior to Mrs. Sponick as a teacher. Perhaps it's because it had taken me some time, and quite a bit of effort, to exhaust Mrs. Sponick's patience, whereas her successor was totally fed up with me in a matter of hours. In other words, Mrs. Sponick had been able to handle all the hijinks and nonsense my young self could dish out; her replacement, by contrast, couldn't even begin to match such incredibly high tolerance levels, a fact which deeply disappointed me.

On this particular day, she took a backseat and let the visitors take the reins. It was "Air Pollution Day," and these visitors were to give a presentation on air pollution and engage with us in various, thematically related skits and activities. With all of us seated at our respective tables, listening restlessly, we were given coloring sheets each of which featured a clown holding a bunch of balloons by a string. Now, you must remember, I was the kid who, whether he meant well or not, would seize any and every opportunity to – how shall we put this? – express his individuality, no matter the likely outcome.

The other kids at my table were all about to start coloring when I blurted out to the group, "I bet you guys don't think I'll draw the clown peeing, do you?" They all looked up from their clown handouts and started to giggle. Of course, I took those laughs as a dare to do just that, and so, never one to shrink from a challenge, proceeded to draw a penis on the clown in approximately the correct anatomical region (and, just for good measure, a commode in front of him).

After we'd all colored and doodled on our sheets for about ten minutes, the visitors giving the presentation began walking from table to table, in a rough circle around the classroom, to judge our progress and provide encouragement where needed. When they arrived at *our* table, their eyes grew as wide as tea-saucers, their jaws gaping as they gazed in horror upon my vulgar creation: a clown, his (no doubt comically oversized) penis, and a five-year-old's crude, hurried depiction of a toilet bowl. One of them immediately seized my handout and – appalled, speechless, aghast, you name it – handed the filth that it was to my teacher. She took one look at the obscenity I had so proudly and clumsily executed, stuffed it hastily into an envelope, and sent it (along with me) down to the principal's office. This incident is the earliest memory I have of being seriously disciplined in kindergarten. (I'm sure I was causing trouble before that; I just can't quite remember what all it entailed, exactly, or what the punishments were.)

Once the principal had learned of my cheeky misdeed and examined my artwork for herself, she sealed it back up in the envelope and gave it to my parents at the end of the school day. If I remember correctly, I think my parents actually laughed at the drawing! Now that I think back on it, I guess it *was* pretty comical. I forgot to mention previously that my kindergarten year was spent at a private Catholic school. The only reason I went there was that my neighbor, who was my best friend at the time, was also enrolled there and was in the second grade. I switched to a public school the next year (or, more accurately, my parents pulled me out of that place). The move, I realize now, was probably for the better. And I'm sure that, after just one year of *me*, the institution had had its fill of young Colin.

Parting isn't always sweet sorrow, I guess. Or sorrow at all, for that matter.

> CHAPTER 3

Beginning in first grade, I became the product of public schools. First grade marked a pivotal time in my younger years, as I underwent a great many changes, some of them quite drastic, in the space of that single year.

It was at some point during first grade, for instance, that I was officially diagnosed as having ADHD and prescribed medication as an initial treatment. I assume the diagnosis was based largely on the impulsivity I'd exhibited throughout kindergarten. I want to reiterate for the record here that, at least in the beginning, my behavior was never malicious in intent. And that changed only when I began to perceive in my interactions with certain adults (mostly my teacher and other staff members) a subtle but unmistakable antipathy toward me, due at least in large measure, I presume, to my "overly" inquisitive and at time mischievous nature. (I wonder sometimes if my awareness of their hostility toward me didn't perhaps spark my early distrust of authority.) Without knowing the exact point in first grade at which I was diagnosed, treated, and medicated accordingly, I can really only speculate that it was probably toward the middle or end of that school year, for that's when the problems really started.

In order for me to tell the story of my becoming medicated and all its unlovely, unintended consequences, I will first need to go back and expand upon the experiences leading up to it, in particular the experience of going to therapy at such a young age. I recall that, in order to be prescribed Adderall, I was required by either law or school policy (or perhaps both) to see the therapist at least once a month. As I look back on it now, the whole notion of being essentially strong-armed into something so psychically taxing as *therapy*, especially at such a tender age (all of six, remember!), really creeps me out. It is a bit disconcerting that educated adults, presumably with

17

my best interests at heart, would have actually thought it prudent to place a child so young into such an emotionally precious spot.

I can still recall how much I despised having to see a therapist back then. I can also still remember the name of the first one who ever analyzed me: Dr. Hipskind. He was middle aged, with an average build and had slicked back longer hair with graying facial hair. His hair wasn't too long, but atleast about almost shoulder length maybe a couple inches above the shoulders. He would always be wearing casual dress shirts with khakis and glasses everytime I visited him. I remember telling him how much I disliked the pills he'd put me on and how I felt so… *different* all of a sudden. Of course he didn't care what I had to say, at least insofar as it conflicted with his agenda (or, if nothing quite so lofty, then at least the conclusions to which he'd apparently jumped on day one); far from discontinuing my meds, he seemed to up the dosage every time I so much as twitched. It got to the point, in fact, that I started keeping a journal in which I described at some length the emotional turmoil into which I'd been thrown (whether by the meds, Dr. Hipskind himself, the whole experience of being in therapy at such a young age, or some combination of these).

Being so young, I had not yet developed much of a vocabulary. Most of the words I'd learned by that point, I imagine I'd learned from my older sister, around whom I spent a good chunk of my early childhood. After each of my first few therapy sessions, I promptly retreated into my bedroom in frustration and anger and took out my little notebook, and to this day I can clearly remember the very first entry I made in it. It read something like this: "I had to see a doctor today, and I don't like him. He makes me take those stupid pills. I hate those little blue pills. They're gay!" (Please forgive my distinctly juvenile and unfortunate word choice there; rather, those were the words of a hurt and confused eight-year-old child with a sixteen-year-old sibling in the '90s, when the given expression was even more widely used by adolescents, mostly innocuously, than it is today.)

The fact that I started documenting my emotions and feelings at such a young age and trying to communicate them in some fashion, although with the inevitable clumsiness of a kid, makes me both proud of and grateful for my much-younger self, in that it shows I was more in touch with my thoughts and emotions than most eight-year-olds (I presume). And recognizing that now, in my late twenties, affords me a great deal of joy. For one thing, it goes to show that self-awareness is within all of us no matter our age; we just need to listen to what we're trying to tell ourselves in order to both identify the questions and comprehend the answers. It is my firm conviction that, from the very beginning of our mental lives, we human beings have access to these important truths about ourselves: we know them intuitively, can readily discover them if only we can sit and be still, and quiet long enough. That way, and *only* that way, can we give ourselves "permission" to know what, unconsciously, we already deep down are aware of. Or so it seems to me, anyway.

First grade was when my parents let my shrink prescribe me a daily dose of Adderall, as they rationalized it, to "help" me focus at school and calm me down. I know now that, at the time, my parents were only doing what they thought would help in a situation that only seemed to worsen over time. They must have been thinking short-term, I suppose, and been rather desperate for a "quick fix" to my behavioral problems (i.e., my highly impulsive conduct, erratic emotions, and seemingly inexhaustible energy and constant distractibility with a touch of chaos).

As soon as I was prescribed my first dose of Adderall, I immediately began to notice its adverse side effects, on my mind and body both. Although the drug did succeed in curtailing some of my more impulsive and reckless behavior, it also quickly took a tremendous toll on my individuality, freedom of spirit and thought, overall happiness, and so on, bit by bit each day. My state of mind quite quickly deteriorated into that of the quintessential "zombie" so feared in the pop culture of modern mood-stabilizers and anti-psychotics. I had achieved, at the absurdly young age of eight, that well-known and exceedingly frightful trade-off: a quieter mind, less restlessness and excitability, in exchange for fewer and less productive manias, fewer wild (and thrilling, and original) thoughts, and significantly less energy, less "electricity" overall.

Each day that I lived and moved within the fog, as I sometimes think of it now – i.e., the semi-stupor in which the meds seemed to leave me nearly all the time - felt hazy and distant, almost surreal, as if it had been lazily sewn together from the previous day. It was as if I were living on a conveyer belt, and stuck to the belt, while it kept moving around and around in the same boring, endless loop, day in and day out. It's enough to make a person feel as if he were going crazy as well as loosing their mind.

When the initial dosage finally took hold, I would often descend for long stretches into what I can only describe as a zombie-like state with absolute complete numbess to the environment around me. I recall feeling by this time more disconnected from people, places, and things - from the world around me, in short – than I ever had previously. I felt so different from my former self, both inside and out, and always as if I were missing out on something (and I suppose I was: the clarity of thought and abundance of energy typical of a normal, healthy child, i.e., precisely the thing the meds should have enhanced rather than dulled).

Worse yet, not once throughout these intense physical and emotional changes did I have an opportunity, really, to relate all the negative side effects the pills seemed to be causing, to describe to any of the grown-ups in my life my ever-growing doubts about the regimen. Or, put more succinctly, about the meds which had been so abruptly and carelessly forced upon me. Not to my parents, not to my teacher, not to my principal – and certainly not to my shrink, the very peddler of the poison that was destroying me. I'm not sure if this was because I felt extremely uncomfortable in the therapy sessions (with a shrink, remember, whom I neither knew nor trusted), or if it was more because Dr. Hipskind didn't seem remotely interested in entertaining my feelings about the matter (no doubt due primarily to my age). Perhaps part of it, at least, was that they already knew the ugly truth about the medication and its usual side effects on kids, and were trying to suppress or ignore it in favor of visible and significant short-term results. It's also quite possible that anyone involved in my prescription of the poison genuinely had no idea of what the side effects were going to be.

By the time each morning's dose of Adderall had fully dissolved in my stomach (usually around lunchtime), taking root in my bloodstream, I would immediately feel any and all positive emotions (happiness, excitement, amusement, etc.), all my positive energy and anticipation of the day ahead, just drain out of me like bath water. I mean, it was as if night and day were trading places, once the daily dosage had fully infiltrated my system. I am most certainly no religious fanatic and don't particularly follow any organized religion, but there is a Bible verse which describes *precisely* how my "soul" felt once I was medicated. "For what shall it profit a man, if he shall gain the whole world, and lose his own soul" (Mark 8:36, KJV). My soul was being lost, all right – forfeited, really – in exchange for brief stints of docile, complacent, compliant behavior. It felt as if someone had just flipped a switch inside me from "ON" to "OFF": that's how drastic the changes felt to me.

All of a sudden, whatever it was inside me that always made me feel so special and different, wasn't inside me any longer. I would feel so numb and placid and basically indifferent to anything anyone would tell me, would say or do in my presence. In the beginning I allowed myself and soul to become compromised, just so people could deal with me better. Such an awful trade-off to have to make – or feel as if you have to make, anyway - at such a young age, don't you think? Luckily this self-imposed arrangement didn't last forever. Nothing is forever, of course, a fact which alternately can be a source of either tremendous relief (e.g., with respect to situational depression and anxiety) or outright terror (e.g., with respect to grappling with one's own mortality).

In the first few weeks of the first grade, just before I was prescribed Adderall, I had a teacher by the name of Mrs. Champagne. She had the benefit of having known "pre-Adderall Colin" quite well before later coming to know, just as well, "post-Adderall Colin." From the very start she had an extremely difficult time understanding and connecting with me. For whatever reason, we both seemed to have it out for one another from the get-go. During my pre-Adderall stage in her classroom, there were a few incidents that stand out in my memory, all of them involving certain patterns of behavior on both her part and mine. One in particular seems to have marked the turning point, the juncture at which it became clear, at least to me, that life with Mrs. Champagne was never going to improve much; if anything, it seemed destined only to deteriorate further. The story to follow should serve well to illustrate my point.

It was the beginning of the school year. The other students and I were all about to line up at our classroom door, single-file, in preparation for the daily lunchtime march to the cafeteria. Of course I didn't get the hint when she first told us all to line up and stand still for a moment while she counted us and opened the door; I was too busy mingling with, entertaining, or simply tormenting my nearby classmates. I would mingle and try to talk and connect with any of my classmates whenver a oppurtunity would present itself. Once it was obvious I was ignoring her command ("Colin! Get in line and stand still, please!"), she came at me with purpose, her arm stretched out in front of her almost as if she were a running back in footbal about to stiffarm her opponent, and clamped her hand down on the back of my neck, personally "re-adjusting" my position in line. This nasty little display of inappropriate and unnecessary aggression, and so early in our student-teacher relationship, quickly dissolved any respect for or trust in her that I might have thus far developed – and, of course, utterly destroyed whatever potential there might have been to grow that trust and respect.

Luckily for Mrs. Champagne (and for me as well, I suppose), she wouldn't have to deal with my unmedicated self for much longer:

before there could be any chance of a prolonged feud between the two of us, I made sure to unleash every bit of my manic and chaotic energy and impulsivity just as often as I could, always eliciting the same predictable and desired reaction from her. With my inexhaustible energy and free-spiritedness also came my trademark straightforwardness of tongue (better known in today's language as "having no filter"). Mrs. Champagne discovered this trait of mine in a most awkward fashion one fateful afternoon in the fall of 1997 .

But first, a little background: as I mentioned earlier, my sister was eight years older than I, which meant I was subjected to "older sibling" behavior on a near-daily basis (especially at nighttime, when I would often hear her talking to her friends on the phone). Courtesy of this fact, although no doubt wholly unintended on her part, I picked up a few choice words and phrases which had no place whatsoever, naturally, in the repertoire of a child of pre-school age or in the classroom.

One afternoon in class, Mrs. Champagne had us kids sit on the floor in a circle while she sat in a chair facing us. I don't remember exactly why we were in a circle or what we were doing, necessarily, but I do recall what happened next. That chaotic impulsivity of mine reared its ugly head once again, bent on wreaking havoc in the usual fashion. I remember raising my hand in the air and waving it eagerly, impatiently back and forth. Mrs. Champagne noticed this, finally, and, most likely with some reluctance, called on me: "Yes, Colin? What is it? What's so important, buddy?" I clearly recall asking her (and yes, this is verbatim), "Mrs. Champagne, why are you wearing black hooker boots?" The boots she was wearing were a cheap, knee-high, faux leather pair with stiletto heels.

I'm not sure if the rest of the class laughed or not, but *I* sure did; I'm certain of *that* much. I laughed, all right: I laughed *plenty*. Immediately after I'd posed to my teacher this decidedly inappropriate query, she pulled me out of the group and isolated me in a chair at a table far away from the other kids. I quickly became all too familiar with the term "the orange chair": it was where she would send me, she explained heatedly, every time I acted out in such a manner. Trust me, she kept true to her word.

Now, in my defense, I am not absolutely sure I even knew the actual definition of the word "hooker" at that age... or maybe I did. Who knows? The important part is that, whatever I knew or didn't know at the time, I did in fact utter the words "hooker boots." I'm also not going to pretend that my sister taught me what such glamorous footwear was or what it looked like. It was just one of those curious associations kids sometimes draw between things while having only the vaguest understanding of the things themselves. I must have drawn this one in my own child-aged mind based on media I'd been exposed to and some of the adolescent slang of which my then-teenage sister sometimes partook (innocently, of course, at least in regards to her baby brother). Everything was so black-and-white to me then, at such a young age, yet so comical to me now, as I look back on it all. I was such an honest kid (in terms of frank communication, at any rate) that I often hurt other people's feelings or bruised their egos, simply as a consequence of telling the truth as I saw it.

As it happened, Mrs. Champagne's final experience with "pre-Adderrall Colin" occurred during a show-and tell moment. This episode didn't reflect any particular behavioral pattern of mine, incidentally; it was just something I did this one time, something I must say seems pretty hilarious in retrospect (as seen through adult "eyes").

Once a week, all the kids would gather round and each child was permitted a few minutes to "show and tell" to the rest of the class. On this particular day I just wanted to do something comical, to get a laugh from my classmates (as you might have inferred by now, I was always something of a class clown). When my turn finally came, I walked to the front of the classroom and sat down in the designated chair, opened a book in my lap. My item of choice to share was a *Captain Underpants* book. On the cover was a cartoon man in his underwear, wearing a red cape and standing on top of a building. It was my absolute favorite series back then to read.

I pointed to the silly looking superhero and stated to the class, "Look, he's only wearing underwear, isn't that funny!" The rest of the kids in my class awkwardly giggled; meanwhile, Mrs. Champagne had apparently reached her limit with me. It seemed I had become, yet again, a disruptive threat to her entire, well-planned-out day. I was a toxic entity rudely and obnoxiously introduced into her otherwise neat, orderly, sanitary environment. It felt like I was being targeted once more, and once more, merely for being myself, annoying as perhaps "pre-Adderral" Colin admittedly could be at times. And heck, it was the first grade, after all: kids in first grade are *supposed* to have lots of energy and imagination (as well as short attention spans). They're also supposed to be mischievous, especially boys, and certainly not always perfectly behaved, either. Right?

Reflecting back to that first year, I see now that it was around this time that my obsessive-compulsive disorder really seemed to take off. To put a finer point on it: the disconnectedness I was feeling and lack of self I was experiencing were now fully manifesting themselves as symptoms of those now-famous three capital letters, an acronym which at the time (the late 90s) was only just entering the popular imagination and lexicon of Western psychology: Obsessive-Compulsive Disorder. I never sought treatment for it as a child; and, indeed, I must confess that, since I was never actually diagnosed with the disorder, I can't be certain that I am afflicted by it in a purely clinical sense. But all the indications were there; my behavior was riddled with all the usual hallmarks of it. It was like a secret I didn't want exposed to the people around me, even though my family did eventually notice the symptoms (long before I would ultimately be told by a doctor what they were symptoms *of*). To this day, I still firmly believe that the OCD, or whatever exactly it was, was a direct side-effect of the Adderall. (My parents used to tell me that they didn't think the two were related, but again, since I never sought treatment for the OCD-like symptoms, we'll never really know.)

Try to sympathize for a moment, if you would, with how I felt back then in those early, precarious days of grappling with these wide-ranging, deep-seated psychological issues, issues which are challenging even for otherwise stable, well-adjusted adults. Going from a child bursting at the seams with so much life, energy, and curiosity to a doped-up mini-zombie who no longer cared about anything, had little or none of his old energy, and didn't seem to care enough to question anything or anyone (or to even think for himself, for that matter): this was one hell of a transition, to put it mildly. (If I might interject a brief PSA at this juncture: I urge anyone who is currently taking or even thinking about taking Adderall, or any of its multiple generic derivatives, to please exercise the utmost caution and discretion, and to exhaust every possible alternative remedy before signing your life over to these soul sucking meds. I assure you: you will thank me later. They will slowly extinguish your beautiful soul and suck you dry of everything that makes you *you*.)

The only thing I seemed to care about in the latter half of my first-grade year was my ever-heightening OCD. It was the only thing I could seem to focus on. It was consuming me more and more on a daily basis. Its growth seemed non-linear, almost exponential on some days. I would find myself stepping back and forth over cracks in the cement, touching the same things in a repetitious manner, and even obsessively looking at the same things over and over again, for no real reason. I know it sounds crazy, but that is what I had to deal with every single day in *elementary school*. Scary stuff for anyone, to be sure, but especially a six-year-old kid.

It was around this time that I started to feel afraid a lot of the time, and lost, and once again "different" from other children my age. I didn't know it at the time (how could I?), but I realize it now: without all these internal struggles, all these baffling hardships of the psyche, I never would have made it to where I am today. I needed all those difficulties, what at the time seemed like gratuitous suffering such as no child (*particularly* no child) should ever be made to bear, in order to find the road to self-discovery, self-honesty, and bona fide spirituality that I now walk, humbly and gratefully, on a daily basis.

Yes, first grade was quite the year for me.

➤ CHAPTER 4

There were two recurring themes with me that I noticed kids and teachers would routinely point out especially around the time I started middle school. One was that I always seemed to ask too many questions, to which my usual reaction was (and remains to this day), "Too many questions? Are you serious?" How can a child, who by definition should be trying to further his knowledge and expand his consciousness of the world around him (and how it works), possibly ask too many questions, particularly those of an academic nature? It's fairly insane to think back on being told that as often as I was. I could never burden my own daughter with such a huge mental and emotional barrier. It would automatically create a certain distance between us, as I assume it also would between a student and his teacher if the student felt the teacher held such a negative attitude toward him, and – this is much more to the point – toward his intellectual curiosity. If you ask *me*, as difficult or aggravating as answering a seemingly endless array of them can be at times (especially those of the "But why?" variety), a child can't ask *enough* questions. Surely, the more questions that my daughter will ask, the more interesting everything in her world is likely to seem.

At a fairly young age it was drilled into me that asking too many questions is not okay and quite annoying, as well as possibly disruptive. It drove me crazy to have what felt like a glass box ceiling over my mind, as well as what felt like the dulling of my senses (partly due, I should add, to the medication I was taking). Sometimes it seemed as if I were struck, every single weekday morning, by this strange sense of impending doom as soon as I walked into school.

I don't know, I may just have a different thought process than most others, but one would think out of common sense that teachers, friends, and family members would be encouraging children to ask as many questions as possible and to always pursue thoughts, not discourage and limit them. From the beginning of middle school onward, because of the limits that were placed on me in the educational system, I already began to feel that all school was doing was indoctrinating me, not teaching me. How are you supposed to take full advantage of the educational system when the ones who are teaching it for the most part won't even let you become yourself in an environment where that is extremely necessary? The Adderall mixed with that type of restricting environment, I know was creating some turmoil deep within my soul and mind.

The second thing that kept popping up in my childhood all throughout grade school to high school was people constantly telling me that I was *too sensitive;* I would be embarrassed then angry with myself every time I would here that phrase. At this point it would be safe to say that I was feeling pretty confused and hurt. When children would tell me I was too sensitive, I would feel weaker than the rest; for some reason I would feel less than. The embarrassment, anger and feelings of weakness combined with the prescription caused me to lose sight of myself in middle school and it showed through my behavior and impulsive acting out.

I need to interject here and let the reader be aware that during kindergarten through a small portion of the first grade I had to wear an eye patch because of my left eye, which has horrible vision. The reasoning being wearing an eye patch at the time was to block my good eye and by only using my bad eye (the left one) that it would make it stronger and be able to see better. That never happened. I am not sure if that is relevant to my story or not but I feel it is an important fact for the reader to be aware of if you are to understand my whole story and my journey towards the truth. Thank god I never needed it in middle school, it would've been too much to handle! I feel the eye patch alienated me even more than I had already felt prior to that point. I remember allowing myself to feel sorry for myself because of my eye patch. That was my first real glimpse into the ever so comforting emotion of sell pity, which would say to me, it's ok to do the things you do because it will make you feel better in a sick and twisted sort of way.

I feel that very well could have been the startup of my trouble making career as a juvenile, which seemed to escalate drastically once middle school hit. It had to have been a way for me to try to shed my identity as the kid with ADHD, who needed to always be on medication to function like a normal kid, to trading that for an identity of trouble making and mayhem. I had to put the "tough kid" mask on so to speak, so it could make up for the "too sensitive" part of me. As far as second grade to fifth grade went, not much happened to me as far as any eye opening moments were concerned.

Now middle school for me took a turn for the worse. I was still on my medication taking more of a daily dose than ever before. My middle school years were full of getting into copious amounts of trouble and defying authority (something that I was very good at from such a young age). In the beginning, I always did seem to care about what others thought of me, but not to the extent of following others.

I have always done my own thing, and have always marched to the beat of my own drum as they say, by any means necessary. By middle school I was feeling extremley detached from the rest of my peer groups. I always seemed to feel a bit different and was always bouncing around from one group to another. I found the best way for me to combat that and connect to people was through my sense of humor and wildness. That always seemed to grab people's attention. I was trapped inside my own skin, nothing I seemed to do could release me from my self. That is when the trouble started happening. It started with arguing with teachers and being defiant then progressing to more serious matters such as vandalizing and alcohol abuse and whatnot.

My behavioral issues stemming from the constant medicated state I was subjected to grow in consistency and strength as the days passed on. Once medicated in middle school I had this need to redefine myself even though the pills were continuing to define me.

The only way I knew how to do this was through acting out and causing trouble.

In the beginning it would often start off as something small, such as coming across argumentative or disruptive, but as the days continuing Adderall increased, so did my behavioral outbursts. It started with me continually being sentenced to lunch detentions. More often than not it was my disruptive or argumentative behavior that earned me a weekly seat in the detention room. On the days I would "forget to take my pills" it would be extra torturous because then I wasn't able to sit numbly through the time period. On those days, I'd be squirming in my chair, the silence killing me as I would watch the seconds on the clock tick by.

I felt so much precious time was wasted inside that lunch detention room, so much missed opportunity and potential sat in that room. Almost as severe as all the lost potential and ideas that sit in the cemetery. But thankfully our ideas and potential are still very much alive still! As each day inside that room passed, I found myself getting more and more angrier within myself, and with the environment around me. After months of consistent detentions, the schools consequences to my actions seemed to increase over time. Up until this point in middle school I had been fairly consistent on having to take the Adderall every morning before class started. There were always a few days that I just would not take them if I could get away with it, or would "forget" to take them in the morning. This incident happened to land on one of those days.

It was early in the morning before class started and all the kids were mingling with one another, just leisurely standing around. Since this was during a day I hadn't taken the medication, I was feeling extremely energetic, rambunctious, and impulsive; so feeling actually quite like myself for once. I met my friend in the hallway that leads to the front of the school, and with him randomly was a pair of dice, so I somehow jokingly convinced him that we should roll the dice and gamble for fun. I told him that I didn't have any money on me, so instead I gambled a stick I had found on the floor. He had a five dollar bill that he put in as a gamble. Now we were twelve year old kids just joking around being silly as such kids are, and right as I was rolling the dice onto the floor the vice principle walked up behind me, and yelled at us to come with him into the principal's office.

He told us that he was going to suspend us for gambling on school property. Remember I wasn't on the Adderall this day so I'm sure I was feeling pretty argumentative towards the vice principle, which reflecting back I'm sure didn't help my case one bit. To get suspended for *pretend* gambling is a bit ridiculous I'd say. I recall the moment he told us that, I started to notice my dislike for authority grow from that point on. My friend and I at the time were suspended for one school week.

That incident stands out to me simply for two reasons. One is that it was the first major incident I got in trouble with when I wasn't taking the Adderall, so I was actually able to feel and be myself for once, and the second reason it stuck out, is because that's when it hit me that I was never going to be accepted for who I truly was meant to be inside of that middle school environment. It was a powerful thought.

It wasn't long after I returned from my mandatory *vacation* that my impulses and lack of respect towards school authority led me to a bit more serious trouble as far as the consequences were concerned.

Being constantly medicated throughout my daily school routine would cause me to feel extreme boredom inside of myself and within the world around me. I was so docile on the stuff that on the rare days that I wasn't on it, I felt I had to make up for *lost time* as they say. I needed an outlet for my creative energy since it was suppressed within the classroom. At the time I had gotten my hands on some magnum sized black permanent markers that I carried with me to school on a daily basis.

At this point I was feeling so creatively vacant and desperate, that I was willing to do whatever I could to express my ideas of what I thought my own identity was. During our lunch breaks while all of the kids were eating their lunch and hanging around one another, I saw that as a perfect opportunity to sneakily retreat into the bathroom and leave my *creative artwork* on display in the bathroom stall.

During this time period of my life I happened to be into graffiti artwork. Although I am pretty confident I only appreciated looking at it, seeing as I have absolutely no artistic talent when it comes to drawing whatsoever. I was only into the action of doing it because it was risky and considered vandalism, so it was a win win for me. It provides an outlet (albeit damaging school property in the process) for my lack of creative energetic impulse that was so denied inside the classroom. It also allowed me a way to feel like I was getting back at school authority by defying the rules of the school. It allowed me to, in a way, finally feel in control of myself and of life somewhat again. Strange way of looking at it but that is how it felt to me.

The first time I went into the bathroom stall and left my *mark*, everything went fine, I got away with it luckily. Eventually I got caught after the third or fourth time of me drawing in permanent marker on the stall. I don't think it would've been so bad if the stalls were already drawn on, but they weren't. They were brand new and the school ended up having to replace a couple panels, since I had kept vandalizing it over and over. So I'm sure they got sick and tired of having to replace it and cracked down on surveillance, while my young self was naive to the fact and was producing a bit of cockiness.

Needless to say I got caught and punished with an *in-school suspension* and after school work hours that I needed to complete within a certain allotted time frame. When my parents caught wind of what had happened, my Adderall dosage increased from what my daily standard had been. When my dosage got increased, it made me feel the need to try and avoid taking it more and rebel more frequently in school out of frustration, confusion, and anger.

The last major incident to happen during my time in middle school, yet again involved vandalism, but this time with higher stakes.

It was during the summer transitioning from the seventh grade to the eighth grade.

During the summer I was still required to take the higher dosage of Adderall prescribed to me, but it was a lot loosely monitored since I wasn't getting up for school and my parents still had to go to work. During the summer times they would take the pills out and leave them on the kitchen counter for me to take upon waking up. As you can imagine it was very easy for me to avoid taking them altogether and just throw them away, which is precisely what I did.

On this day I avoided taking the Adderall like a fat kid does broccoli, and plotted what crazy, fun, and creative activities I could conjure up that day. At the time I had a handful of cans of spray paint in a plastic bag hidden in my bedroom, which I decided to take those, as well as my dog, to my middle school and spray paint one of the buildings walls. Now there was obviously no forethought to that plan and I let my impulsiveness take control, since that is what it did best at the time.

When I arrived on the scene, I chose the back of the gymnasium wall to leave my mark. I was maybe only 2-3 minutes in at most of spray painting the wall with my *artwork* when the same school faculty member who caught me the previous year turned the corner and caught me red handed in the middle of spray painting. He immediately told me that the police were on their way and to follow him inside. Right when he told me that, I grabbed my dogs leash with him attached (since he came with me to participate) and took off sprinting through the woods, bee lining it back to my house since no one was home, they all were still at work. Reflecting back it was foolish to run, as I am sure my address and phone number were all on file with the school, so that information could easily be exchanged to the police to pursue the incident I was now involved in.

Obviously I got caught and my parents were called at work and had to come home and talk to the policeman about my foolish actions. This time I was sentenced to more community service hours and a fine I had to pay off over time for my vandalism I committed.

It's quite interesting to note that as my dosage increased so did my bad and defiant behavior; it's as if they went hand in hand with one another. Needless to say I am sure my parents were feeling extremely frustrated and desperate at this point, and as well as I to be completely honest. At least it was safe to say that my spray painting days had finally come to an end.

From that point on, all throughout high school and even a little beyond, it was a constant game for me every day to try to avoid taking the Adderall by any means necessary. I had frequent small glimpse into what it felt like to feel like myself again, I craved it.

The only issue was then to learn how to control, manage, and direct my energy and behavior into productive, constructive processes while maintaining off the Adderall instead of getting wild and showing the adults they were right all along in a way. That eventually came in time, even though it took me years and countless troubles, but then again, I've always felt that the truth is worth finding at all costs.

➤ CHAPTER 5

In my first two years of high school, on the days I would have to take the Adderall, I would sit down and be quiet all throughout class. All day long, in fact, or so it seems now in my memory of the time. I specifically remember how all the other kids would notice something was seriously different with me. I was no longer the loud, funny, rebellious kid; instead, I became quiet, withdrawn, the docile and obedient kid, as passive and malleable as a straw in the wind. It was if the meds were basically shaping my late-adolescent identity *for* me.

I didn't even care about living life; the excitement and passion I usually had, ostensibly had vanished into thin air once again. That is a very powerful and disturbing thing to feel in high school, the fact that partly how people viewed me was because of my identity of who I became while taking the medication, meaning how they saw me act and change was how they associated me with the Adderall. Very confusing times for myself to navigate through, no wonder so many troubles arose along the way.

I remember I would wake up to get ready for high school in the morning and immediately when I saw those pills I would get a feeling of dread deep inside my stomach knowing very well that soon I would have to succumb to the identity it gave me by making me feel and act completely different. The days I wouldn't take it, I'd be so elated that I would almost brag to my classmates about how I didn't and how I felt so great, happy, and hyper. The teachers on the other hand weren't as happy when those days would roll around. High school must've just been the final straw, but even in grade school through middle school I vividly remember feeling like I was giving up a piece of my true self for a piece of something synthetic to cause a temporary fix, while being completely unknown to the long term side effects. It's mind blowing what society will go through, to place upon children the idea of even being a bit disruptive and questioning is absolutely not ok in the educational system and must be repressed at all costs.

I could never understand why the teachers couldn't change their own way and approach of dealing with a higher caliber of energy than the average kid in class. It's quite possible they just didn't care enough to try anything else, or quite simply they just didn't want to deal with it. Either way you look at it, I still feel connection and communication is key to any breakthrough. But why try any harder than the paycheck demands, right? Especially when it comes to the public school system. So sad, but the good news is, the identity, pain and restriction that came with it did not last forever. Which is absolutely a beautiful thing. The journey is beautiful. Without the journey there isn't even a destination; without a destination there is no vision; and without a vision there is no future. Everything starts with the journey. In the final analysis, the journey itself is *everything*.

I allowed other people to craft my identity for me, to *assign* me an identity, as it were. I was so worn-out with the medication, I didn't even realize the power I was giving up. My limited vision of the future didn't help me either. I couldn't see past that day, my mind was so cloudy from the Adderall, it allowed me to focus on emptiness in school rather than richness and thoughtfulness at the expense of my normal high functioning mind, if that makes any sense to the reader. It was easier to be what everybody expected me to be than to forge my own path (which I eventually did, thank god). Existence throughout high school was a mixture of blending in when I should've stood out, and standing out when I most certainly should have blend in. The chaos soon followed me wherever I went. I continued my acts of defiance and argumentative behavior throughout the schooldays, but high school was a drastic year of change for me as far as the medicating went. It was during one of those years I was soon to live life while going completely off the pills. It took time, but as anything worth having in life, usual does.

Up until high school, I had no real familiarity with spirituality, hadn't even touched the tip of it other than my foolishness attempts of portraying an image like I somehow knew what I was talking about (I had and still to this day have no concept of spirituality other than how I feel and react to people and situations around me). This path was guiding me towards the beginning stages of attempting to shed the identity I allowed others to place on me, which I then allowed myself to adopt. So wrong of me, wasn't it?

It was during my junior year of high school that I finally put my foot down and refused to take so much as another single dose of Adderall. It had continually wreaked havoc upon my mind, body and soul for 10 or more years. That's over a decade of medication I felt I never should have taken in the first place. When I put it into yearly form like that it has a bit more of an impact on myself reflecting back; that's a very long time to not be who you were truly meant to be. Of course, it was going to take just as long, if not longer to learn how to function at my base line again, and reintegrate back into society.

The first few months of high school after I quit the Adderall, I was filled with energy, excitement, and passion. I'm not exaggerating when I say that I felt brand-new again. I was no longer waking up with a sense of impending doom which lingered throughout my day. My natural interests and curiosities returned seemingly overnight, restored in full force. The first few months were tough as far as behavioral transition and rebalancing went, but for my mind and soul, the trip was smooth sailing. I can't even tell you how refreshing it was to feel like my old self again.

At first I was reprimanded almost constantly for my disruptive conduct. Usually this amounted to little more than my whispering – okay, sometimes just plain *talking* – to a classmate while the teacher was lecturing. (Mostly harmless, yes, but also somewhat distracting, I'll admit.) I wanted to learn on my own by connecting with others on an individual level. I think that's why I would talk to everyone in class and wander in my focus so rapidly and indefatigably from person to person, thing to thing; I craved meaningful relationships with people and places alike (the fact that I had just spent roughly a decade entirely *disconnected* from everyone and everything around me might have had something to do with it; you could say I was making up for some pretty substantial lost time).

The hard part at first was learning how to manage and control my impulsive behavior, which I didn't do such a great job at in the beginning. Also what helped was the fact that my parents were threatening to make me take the Adderall again if I couldn't learn to control myself in school. That aided in pushing me to grow. It was all mostly trial and error, just like anything in life tends to be when trying to progress.

To work on actively trying to outgrow my ADHD identity, took patience and a copious amount of grit and determination. How do you rebuild on a life that has been masked from you for so long? The journey was challenging and still is quite difficult at times but finally finding the path that leads me in the correct direction was a pleasant surprise.

Up until this point it felt as if I was trying to swim upstream and was going nowhere. I had so many unanswered questions, so much unused potential, and craving a vision. I just couldn't get it out of my head. When the medication ceased it felt as if I was swimming with the current for once, not against it. It felt so natural and right.

The difficult part was discovering truth again after living a decade of lies. Once off the medication I had extreme difficulty in trusting people. I didn't know who I could trust. My whole environment at times would feel hostile to my mind. The whole time this transformation was occurring, I produced on the outside, this image that everything was fine and going smoothly, when in fact I was panicked and chaotic at times. As I mentioned earlier it was as if I was putting a "tough guy" mask on in an attempt to cover up my insecurities and fragility I felt I was experiencing.

The truth has a way of coming up to the surface of your life when you allow it and continue to ask the right questions. I had no trouble with the question part of the journey, only allowing me to come across it was difficult at times. No matter where I went or what I did the truth was soon to follow me.

The growth I experienced during the first two to three years of completely off the Adderall was a beautiful and wonderful thing. As I stated earlier I needed to learn how to control myself and mind first in order to continue on my path towards growth. It was absolutely necessary I started managing myself and emotions first, before all the real changes and growth could occur. It took a few months of extreme trial and error with my behavior immediately getting off the Adderall, but once I learned how to manage myself, the rest just seemed to always fall into place. It's like I finally tuned into my correct frequency of living and life. I use the word manage and not master because I may never master my own self, that's a daily discipline that must continue throughout my whole life, and when I say *manage* I could barely do that at the time. I managed my behavior off the pills just enough so I wouldn't get in trouble or caught.

In the beginning of this transition to not taking any medication at all, I specifically remember a few random children in my high school would come up and ask me if I did or didn't take my pills that day, mostly, I think just to judge if I was going to be funny and entertaining in class for them or dull and boring. Feeling that sort of speculation into my own personal life felt very strange and awkward.

Even though I wasn't taking the Adderall any longer, a small part of that familiar feeling of disconnectedness was still looming around my brain throughout the beginning days. As I said earlier my soul and mind felt great once off the pills, it was my environment and how I would continually react to it, most of the time with a negative manner. It was as if I was holding resentment towards the environment to which I usually detested. Mostly due to how the authority figures within would react to my behavior.

There were two incidents that stood out to me as far as impact and growth towards my actions went. One of these teachers I honestly didn't even particularly like or even get along with, but she saw the truth within me and was good at reminding me. Her name was Dr. Bishop and I had her as my teacher both during taking the Adderall and also when I got off and stopped taking it. She was able to see the polar opposites it produced within me almost side by side.

It was during one of the days I had recently stopped taking the Adderall, that she made a statement to me that quite possibly changed my thought process. I was feeling extremely hyper and impulsive that day in her class since I hadn't quite learned how to manage my new sense of personal freedom, since it was all so new to me. It was the usual talking to a classmate while she was talking, and disrupting the class that brought her attention upon me. She told me that when the bell rings, I was to remain seated at the table and talk to her for a bit.

The bell rang and I remember the orchestrated sound of all the chairs being slid out at the same time and the massive rustling of feet as the kids hurried out the door, everybody except me. That instantly caused me to have extreme anxiety. The important aspect to this is that she came up to me with a calm smile on her face and pulled up a chair and sat next to me. I remember it like it happened very recently, she then looked at me and said, "Colin, you are the type of person that's either going to be dead or in jail, or the president of the united states." that statement was powerful to me, I didn't show it at the time but later when I had a chance to reflect on it, it had sustenance to it.

That statement of hers very well could have repositioned my outlook on life indefinitely. If anything it made me pause even for a brief moment and reflect upon my behavior and how I react to situations in class and to the world around me. It was the first time since being off the Adderall that I felt a person with authority saw who I truly was and what I could become only if directed in a productive manner. It was a bit exhilarating to feel that split second of a very meaningful moment in life in a public school none the less. As I stated earlier, I still never really got along with that teacher but I did learn to respect her within her classroom from that point forward.

The second experience that has been embedded into my memory was that of a teacher I had by the name of Mark W. He always told us to call him by his first name, which really helped me to break through the authority's dislike I seemed to always carry. It was a neutralizer of sorts; it brought him down to our level it seemed. He had a way of neutralizing any situation or conflict on the spot and on a whim, while remaining in control of the classroom the best he could (for the most part) and constructively criticizing a kids behavior in a non-patronizing manner. I got the sense that he really, truly cared about us, his students for the most part. Looking back I'm a bit disheartened at how much in the beginning I took advantage of his kindness inside the classroom. It truly does make me sad to think how much I took advantage of that level of patience and kindness in a teacher. Those traits seem to be so rare these days inside of the educational system.

For the most part I would goof off and talk to the other kids during assignments and presentations, listening to and learning nothing while gossiping like a 13 year old school girl, with complete disregard to my surroundings and environment.

What Mark taught me through his actions and communication is still, to me, priceless. It too may have most certainly changed my life. He may very well be the first person to bring to my attention, my own self-awareness regarding my own disruptive behavior. Whenever I would be totally off task and talking and not paying attention, he would never lose his temper towards me or anyone else and he would always so clearly and precisely ask me why I was being so rude and disruptive. Then he would politely and calmly ask me to please try not to talk as much while he was talking.

His patience and his humble ability to grab my attention and reflect on my own behavior, causing me to see where I was wrong and try to grow from that, is a lesson of great importance to myself. The way he conveyed it to me was magnificent. For the first time I paused and truly reflected upon my classroom behavior and actions, which then presented to me my own flaws, which I immediately

43

wanted to start working on for my own personal development. I am forever grateful for that life lesson, thank you Mr. Wright.

➢ CHAPTER 6

"The prideful, rational mind, comfortable with its certainty, enamored of its own brilliance, is easily temped to ignore error, and to sweep dirt under the rug." That is an excerpt from Jordan B. Peterson's most recent book *12 Rules for Life*.

That was me when I got off the Adderall completely. I ignored all past errors and didn't care to take the time to try to heal and learn in the beginning. It's as if I grew cocky once off it and didn't bother cleaning up my past or even my own mind for starters.

Since I wasn't dealing with my past issues, and leaving them unresolved, I allowed it to present itself through more self-anguish and bad choices. You see in the initial four months or so of quitting the Adderall I decided I wasn't going to tell my family I was quitting, because I knew my parents wouldn't be happy at first, so I figured in the meantime before I could actually convince them to let me stop taking the medication, that I would trade my daily dose for cash at first.

I can tell I allowed my unresolved issues from my past to remain untouched at that point because I was trading them for cash, and deep down it felt like a way for me to get back at all the people who thought I should take it in the first place. If I honestly was dealing with those past issues immediately, then I don't feel I would have had the necessary need to be dishonest and not take my medication, and trade them for cash. It was a way of getting even, although the only person I ever got even with was myself in a strange way. I recall the feeling of self-satisfaction I got every time I didn't take the Adderall and instead sold them to the football players and students at my high school. It was exhilarating. It was never a lot, just my daily allotted amount, but I was able to save them up over time and save up my profits during the upcoming four months.

After a few months of keeping that up, I soon grew tired of doing the transactions. I think mostly it was due in part to the fact that I felt I couldn't keep up with the dishonesty and deceitfulness. Everytime I made a transaction I would always feel as if something were about to go horribly wrong. It was my first time ever dealing with something like that and I soon grew weary of it all and instead allowed myself to become more so distracted.

Cockiness and my lack of love towards authority, led me down a path of a new form of self-medication. In the early stages of stopping the medication, once I quit the Adderall, without even realizing it at first, I switched over to the self-medicating technique for quite some time. I replaced the Adderall with cannabis and alcohol for the very first time. Those two substances both seemed to keep me distracted from focusing upon myself (which is what I was aiming for then) and in doing so, solving all my so called problems then, or so I thought. I was very much so wrong.

Before I ever completely quit taking the Adderall I had tried cannabis for the first time when I was around the age of thirteen or so. I feel that was mostly in part to my already predisposed and impulsive behavior, back when I would stop taking the Adderall for only a day or two in middle school. The consistent self-medication use of it for me didn't develop until high school once I was off the medication for good.

My first experience with cannabis, though, during my thirteenth year, was memorable and intense. To this day I can replay the scenario of that day in my head, as if it had just happened. Some friends and I had just left school for the day and were headed to a friend's birthday party. To get to the friend's house where it was to be held, we had to walk through a beautiful, wooded park with large maple trees standing guard over the winding gravel path that wove its way through them. While we were ambling along this path, one of my friends stopped and pulled out his pipe. I, meanwhile, produced the cannabis I'd gotten my hands on somehow earlier that week.

The first puffs I had ever taken were harsher than I had possibly imagined. As with most first-timers, I thought I was going to cough myself to death and not be able to catch my breath. I felt as if the coughing lasted an eternity. I was grasping for air with every breath I tried to take. The more I tried to breathe normally, the harder I ended up coughing.

What I experienced soon after the coughing subsided, may have also had a big influence on my life and how I view it. It was an experience I will never forget. Once the coughing ceased I immediately started to feel cerebral pressure around the top of my head and a heavy but yet seemingly lite pressure behind my eyeballs. After growing comfortable with that feeling for what felt like a few short minutes, maybe seconds, I felt myself leaving my body and watching myself from above walk through the park. It was a complete out of body experience for me the first time I smoked cannabis. Right as I was leaving my body and watching myself I remember feeling calm and relaxed, but once I started to think about what I was seeing and what I was experiencing, I quickly started to feel my anxiety rise and panic set in. Now reflecting back to my first cannabis experience, I feel the panic may have set in due to the fact I felt like I didn't have control of myself for a brief moment, but now realizing, I was always in control during that experience it was just the unknown that I allowed myself to become anxious over, even to this day at times.

As I mentioned earlier, cannabis didn't become a self-medication for me until I was in high school and off the Adderall for good. Once off the medication, I needed to jump into something else because that was how I operated for the last few years in order to distract me from myself. Even though as I learned, trying to distract yourself from one's self, only leads you back towards yourself. It's quite funny how it works out I've come to notice.

If I am to discuss my self-medication techniques in place of the Adderall to the reader than I also must reflect back to my first experiences with alcohol as well if I am to communicate only truth to you all.

The self-medication with alcohol didn't start until high school as well. All the distractions of my past and built up frustration towards the Adderall all seemed to disappear once I began drinking alcohol and feeling its effect on me. At first it was a way for me to rebel and stand out and continue my defiance towards authority. Little did I know, that all of that would be the beginning of a downward spiral in my life, well my whole life hasn't been a downward spiral, especially now currently, but when I look back on all those post Adderall years I really notice how far I fell off track. I became obsessed with the idea of getting outside of myself and always feeling the need to alter my state of mind. For some reason once off the medication, I constantly felt like I needed to not feel normal, whatever that may have meant to me back then at the time. I looked at normal as weak or boring. Such a distorted and limited perception I was seeing through.

The drinking didn't start out habitually self-medicating for me until the end of my high school career. Matter of fact, the first few instances involving me drinking I remember becoming extremely ill due to the fact I had never drank alcohol prior to that point.

My first time experimenting with alcohol was in the end of middle school while I was still prescribed the Adderall; the self-medicating didn't set in until completely off the prescription. I remember waiting for my parents to fall asleep upstairs and then after an hour or so of waiting I tip-toed up the small flight of stairs to the kitchen were my father kept a large plastic bottle of cheap London's dry gin in the cupboard above our refrigerator.

I took two or three shots of that foul stuff for the first time ever and felt as if my throat was burning from fire. It was horrible to say the least, but the effects at the time I grew to admire and desire. Once off the Adderall, I started to continually self-medicate with it; I started to take pride in my drinking. As an adolescent I would often brag to another friend or classmate of mine about how much I could drink, and how everyone else wasn't as *cool* as me, or just couldn't *keep up* with me, whatever that was supposed to mean. Wow was I so wrong in every sense of the way reflecting back.

Reflecting back on my situation and environment I can see how distorted my vision of it all was. I was entering quite possibly one of the biggest growth periods of my life and through a portion of it, drowned it out with the constant use of alcohol, because to focus on myself instead and think about my future was absolutely not an option at the time; I'm not quite sure why though. Quite possibly I just didn't want to take the time to invest in myself, possibly out of fear of what others may have thought of me or fear of rejection or just fear of the unknown. I didn't want to ask myself the right questions because deep down I wasn't ready for the answers I presume. The universe has a funny way of leading you to where you need to go, even if you think you're not quite ready.

In the early years of high school, as my medication decreased and went away, my bad behavior and crime wave picked up and increased. Thankfully that ratio didn't last forever.

➤ CHAPTER 7

Upon entering my first year of high school un-medicated I was a wreck. Although I didn't always feel like one, nor would I have ever admitted to feeling like one either. This is when the pace of it all started to pick up rather quickly with myself.

I vividly remember getting ready for the first day of high school, walking down towards my bus stop early in the morning, and since I lived in a quiet, small and secluded neighborhood, no one else was outside with me at the time, just me, my thoughts and my detrimental behavior and chaotic thought patterns. It was the perfect time for me to reach into my backpack and withdraw my water bottle that was halfway full of gin I had taken the night prior, and took a big huge chug of the fowl stuff, then I finished up with smoking a bit, all this before the bus came to pick me up at 7:15 Am.

Looking back that was definitely a warning sign; it was a scream for help. I was on the opposite end of the spectrum showing complete lack of self-control already before my first day of class. It was as if I was on a train with no brakes only gaining momentum while trying to slow down, but being able to do nothing about the speed at which you are traveling because there are no brakes!

The truth of the matter is I did have my own brakes all along; I just lacked the knowledge and self-discipline to apply them in my younger years. As you can imagine my un-medicated behavior only escalated in the beginning months of high school, it was free to roam and test out the waters unfortunately. My bad behavior and crime spree only started to gain traction after that first day of high school. It was as if I had found the secret formula to be able to make it through the day (or so I thought). Although I was only a kid I don't know what could have been so bad and painful that even at that age I felt the need to alter my mind state and escape as soon as possible almost on a daily basis just to feel like I could make it through a full school day. Once again, a lot more warning signs trying to get my attention, and I failing to even notice them as such. At least I notice them now, I suppose that is better than a lifetime of ignorance.

As time progressed so did my uncertainty for the future. Since I had gotten away with alcohol and cannabis use on my first day, deep down that almost *encouraged* me in a way to continually try and self-medicate myself every day before, during and after school. I suppose because at first I had gotten away with it, and if I didn't get caught then of course I felt like it was a good idea to continue, without even stopping to think about the fact that maybe going to school every single intoxicated and under the influence wasn't such a great idea at all, and in the long term, quite detrimental to my school and home life. I was becoming cocky yet again, with my defiance toward authority in general. Sooner or later it was going to catch up with me, I just was nowhere near ready to start to get and hear the message. As they say "it takes what it takes". I was blind to the fact. Very ignorant of my own behavior and its consequences on people and myself.

My un-medicated behavior took a turn for the worse (no surprise there) which led me to my first (and not my last) experience with law enforcement within the school system environment. My whole aim wasn't to attract the attention of school authority and police, matter of fact I didn't want to hurt anyone else from my behavior, I only wanted to get outside of my own self and mind but in the process faced the consequences associated with my impulsive behavior and actions.

My first week of high school off the Adderall was extremely bumpy and rough to say the least for myself. It was during one of our lunch breaks that I had decided to cross the street with my friend and head into the woods to smoke some cannabis. Now if I had only stayed there for a few minutes instead of a whole 40 minutes the outcome of this story may very well have played itself out differently, but that's neither here nor there and it most certainly did not, and I stayed smoking in the woods for the whole duration of the lunch break.

While towards the end of my smoking session, right as I was about to pack my things up and head back to the school, I witnessed the school security guard sneak up on my friend and I and catch me red handed while I was in the middle of smoking out of the pipe.

This was a very surreal moment for me as I had never gotten into any legal trouble involving my substance use up until this point, and it didn't help the fact that I was extremely high from sitting there smoking so much during my lunch break! I could feel the fear and panic set in within me instantaneously. As soon as the school security guard spotted us, I hurled the pipe behind me off into the woods. That obviously didn't do a single thing to help my situation out since he saw the whole thing. He just told me to keep my hands in my pockets and he went and retrieved the pipe. Once he grabbed it he had me walk back with him towards the school and into the principal's office where the school police officer and principle were both awaiting my arrival.

I was terrified, I was sure my current actions were going to land me right back on the Adderall that I so desperately tried getting off in the first place. I'll never forget my parents having to come down to pick me up and witnessing the look of horror and disappointment within my mother's face. She looked so sad that her son was making those choices at such a young age it seemed to me. I vividly remember seeing her cy on the car ride home she was so disappointed and shook.

In the scheme of my life that incident by no means was the end of the world or even a really big deal as far as impact on my future went. It is a bit comical to look back and relive how powerful my emotions were then of fear. When it was happening it felt like close to the end of the world for me, but know I don't put much thought into it at all other than when I was giving it thought to put into this book, so strange. The way my mother took it though, I could have sworn it seemed like the end of the world. I suppose that is why it still sticks with me in my memory so vividly. No child wants to cause their own mother pain and sadness.

The consequences produced from my actions were a bit more serious though then what I was accustomed to in the past seeing how this was the first time I was involved with the juvenile legal system. I was suspended from high school for 2 weeks and sentenced to 20 hours of community service as punishment for the actions I committed.

Before my suspension was over I had talked my parents into switching me to the other high school in town so I could be closer with my friends. At this point in my life I was feeling quite a bit of anger and frustration still, mostly in part that I felt as if everyone was still out to get me or they didn't understand *who* I truly was. Honestly, at the time I don't think I even knew who I was, but I sure thought I did back then.

The change of schools had no immediate effect on my behavior. Now I was just surrounded with more of my friends and still not taking the Adderall, it was a recipe for success in my mind (a disaster in other minds). The trouble with the law didn't stop at the first school; I can assure you that it did follow me to the next high school as well.

This time because of my impulsive behavior I would encounter my first real experience with the police. It was during our lunch break, I had talked one of the older kids sitting next to me in art class by the name of Gino, to drive me in his car while we smoked a joint in it. Since I was providing the cannabis he agreed to be the driver. As soon as I got inside of his car, before we even started driving off I impulsively lit the joint with complete disregard to my surroundings. (Cocky a bit?) Gino, the driver, didn't come to a complete stop at the stop sign before turning right and immediately after turning a sheriff was behind us watching the whole thing. As I was inhaling the smoke from the joint I saw the sirens light up and start flashing behind us. I panicked and threw the joint out of the window.

Once we pull over and he takes us out of the car I immediately take full and all responsibility for the cannabis. I was terrified; I thought for sure I would end up in juvenile detention. I forgot to mention earlier that while all this was happening my parents were out of town on a vacation for a triathlon race my mother was going to compete in. Once the cop handcuffed me and threw me into the back of his car I had to wait a good 20 minutes before he came back. He called my parents even though I told him they were not in town, and then after telling them what I had done, he had me call my grandma who was watching me at the time to come pick me up. Bless her beautiful heart and soul, she passed away last year.

I was allowed to go grab my things from school and then go straight home, instead of having to go to juvenile detention. I suppose I dodged a bullet on that one. As time off the Adderall increased so did my troublesome behavior. I felt that sooner or later I somehow needed to get a grip on it; I just could not manage to continually do so.

My punishment for the cannabis possession the second time increased in severity as well. This time my community service hours doubled and I was now to report to the juvenile probation officer for the next six months.

It was during this time period that my drinking increased and took off dramatically, I would try to drink every day that I could get away with. I could not smoke for the next six months due to the random urine analysis test I was subjected to from the probation officer. Since I could not smoke all my attention and focus went towards the alcohol. To me that was all there was and all there ever was going to be. I could not see anything past that without being able to smoke cannabis. Once again, another period in my younger life where I was exhibiting an extremely limited vision for myself and future

I started to become more disconnected emotionally from people around me and started putting on a show. As in show I mean never letting anyone get to close to me and to get to know the real me.

This is around the time I started to consistently self-medicate with alcohol.

All along the feeling of disconnectedness and feelings of being different were all fears and assumptions made up in my own head to justify my current behavior at the time to myself, and allow myself to continue what I was doing. It was nobody's fault, except my own, and the pre conceptions i had of myself limiting my growth forward.

➢ CHAPTER 8

Right around the time I started going to the second high school, (the one I graduated from) my family sold the house and moved to the other side of town where they had bought a smaller home then the one we had previously lived in. This was my first time moving in fifteen years so it was a big exciting change, which caused me to have even more excitement and energy build up within myself than I already had to begin with.

Every street within a 5 mile radius ended with wood: *cherry wood, cedar wood*, etc., so me and my friends living in the neighborhood started referring to it as the *wood hood* as a brainless joke. Moving over there provided me a lot more freedom to roam around outside and explore my impulses, since I now lived closer to more of my friends and was more of a open neighborhood by a shopping center, not so closed off and secluded like the cul-de-sac house I lived in prior. I was doing things I wasn't supposed to be doing and running into all sorts of different people and it was happening a lot more in my new environment than it was in my old one.

Once I was settled into my new home on *cedarwood ave.,* I soon resorted back to my vandalism and acts of defiance. Once again my actions at first didn't subside due to the move, they only increased with frequency and severity. Now I had more time and freedom to run around with my friends un-medicated causing all sorts of mayhem.

The increase of continually bad behavior on my part was due to the fact that firstly, I still had not mastered how to manage and control my impulses, and secondly because I still lacked my true identity, and in the process I continually allowed my peer groups and friends to place their identity's of who they thought I was onto myself and allowed those thought patterns to define my character. No wonder

I never was truly happy. The whole process was insane and extremely taxing.

It was as if I was a puppet being controlled by the strings attached to me, when all I had to do was to cut the strings loose from myself and re learn how to operate on my own accord, strength, and individuality.

Shortly after moving over towards the north side of the town onto *cedarwood*, I was introduced to my first ever experience regarding psychedelics. By the time summer had rolled around I was experimenting with mushrooms with my other friends from the neighborhood. We had all summer to experiment and wander around at times aimlessly. but at the same time with a slight sense of purpose, even if it was directed towards mischief in the beginning.

After the initial fun and excitement began to wear off, I began to notice that after my mushroom experiences I would become a bit more self-aware of myself and of my surroundings each time I was finished. Surely it was due to the fact that I would still be processing what I had just witnessed and experienced. I would feel more self-aware of myself, that also meant I was a bit more conscious and aware of my actions and behavior. I was starting to notice how my words and actions were affecting the people around me at all times.

In the beginning I didn't spend much time reflecting upon my new perspective, but as the time went on, I spent more time coming back to the idea of self-awareness, and how truly important that is when it comes to aligning myself with the truth and communicating my truths. Without the awareness, the truth would never become visible to me, and if the truth never became present to me then I would not be here communicating it to you all. After a few psychedelic mushroom experiences during that summer I started to spend a bit more time upon reflecting exactly why was it that I decided I needed to get off the Adderall for good in the first place. Up until this point I had not spent much, if anytime at all really asking myself that question and trying to dig deep for answers within. It was all so new to me, this process of growing and improving upon every aspect of my life. It was extremely intimidating at first but once the rhythm was set and I started to see small results I became hooked, almost obsessed like.

It was at this point that I understood and realized that I could not rush this journey. To rush would mean that I would only be rushing myself and neglecting the small important details and lessons in the process. Everything in the past had to happen exactly the way it was meant to happen in order for me to continue through the journey and end up at this current conclusion I was seeing of myself. It was like I could see a little wider in my vision of life; not much wider, but a bit more than the last 10 years leading up to that point, and that was much better that nothing I came to understand.

In the beginning it felt like I wanted to get off the Adderall just so my friends would like me better. It still was connected to this idea that I was doing it to fit the identity others had of me rather than for my own self. I'm not sure why at first I was so attached to the identity others had of me, it was hard to get rid of that mentality and fear, but I did and I want the reader to know that it is possible to live out your own idea of who you are not the idea of others, very important. As time went on this theory proved not to be true because I found within myself that my own personal reasoning for stopping the medication had finally surfaced within me.

After spending some time pondering those questions within myself I came up with a few answers. First and foremost I had to quit the Adderall so I would be able to obtain my soul back. The way Adderall robbed me of myself slowly over a period of time, is excruciating to think back upon, it absolutely was not sustainable for long periods of time. Quite simply, the soul wants what the soul wants, and the soul will get what the soul deserves. I knew that my soul deserved more, so much more. With each passing day it was being caged piece by piece.

I remember asking myself towards the end of my use of the medication, how am I ever going to honestly be myself when I constantly would feel restricted from the pills. My soul was sending me warning signs in the form of early self-awareness. I was not even really aware of the fact that I was doing a self-analysis subconsciously of my own conscience in a way.

When you make a decision based off certainty it is amazing how quickly your life can and will change, either for the better or for the worse. The fact that such a medication can manipulate and rob you of your soul should be deemed highly dangerous and approached with extreme caution. I feel if otherwise, then it has the potential to take over your very own being, and once that happens, what used to make *you, you,* is no longer present.

I feel the opposite is true when it comes to diagnosing and prescribing children for ADHD. The terms and symptoms so loose almost anyone can and does fall under that category. It makes one think if that was a system designed purposefully for that very reason. What better way to numb down the population by telling children they need medication since they fall into the category of ADHD and justifying the fact because of children's inability to focus and stay on task at times. It truly is preposterous.

According to The American Psychiatric Association, (APA) in 2013, "5% of children have ADHD" and according to the CDC's website "approximately 9.4% of children 2-17 years of age (6.1 million) had ever been diagnosed with ADHD, according to the parent report in 2016" (CDC.gov)

As one can tell from that percentage, the number of children diagnosed with the disorder is extremely high – and so is the average dosage of medication being administered accordingly. In 2016 it was reported by the CDC that "among children with ADHD, 62% of them [regularly take] ADHD medication." So, nearly two-thirds of the roughly 6.1 million children in this country already diagnosed with ADHD have already suffered serious spiritual dilution, or stand at serious risk of same, all that they might better conform to society's rigid notion of how children should think, look, and behave. Tragically, no doubt many of these children will never recover, will never see their true, unfettered personalities restored – and, more tragically yet, will never know any differently. They will be zombies for life.

If my reasons for getting off the medication came to me without searching in the beginning, then I know there are people out there who surely must be feeling the same way I did almost thirteen years ago as of the time of this writing. There is, at least, *some* good news for them: it does not have to be this way forever, and you *do* have a choice in the matter, as difficult as that might be to believe in the moment. If, over time, *I* was able to learn how to manage my behavior and utilize my "disorder" to my advantage, then anyone in a similar situation could undoubtedly do the same, if only with some effort and determination. I need you to believe, dear reader – indeed, to *know* – that such deprogramming (or "relearning," if you like) is perfectly feasible.

Right up until the point that I decided to quit the medication, I had come to the conclusion that it was having negative effects on my mind as well as my spirit. That was one of the things I had to take into account when deciding to quit the Adderall. Do you remember when growing up how all the adults would tend to mention how drugs and alcohol, if taken to far, would rob you of your goals and dreams? Well the Adderall had that affect on my mind without the help of other drugs and alcohol. The other conclusion I came up with in regards to putting down the Adderall during my brief introduction to a bit of self-awareness I was experiencing, was that I honestly decided that, if I wanted to grow again in this life, then I needed to be able to think for myself and discover and work toward my goals again. My mind needed to be clear, not cloudy, that was crucial for my growth. I could do none of that while on the medication. It was as if each day I was taking the Adderall my vision of my future seemed to get a bit more distant, as well as dimmer.

Prior to that, growing up I always seemed to be so goal and task oriented. You did not have to encourage or remind me to accomplish and set goals. I loved attacking each waking day with enthusiasm and vigor. It was part of what made me. I always had tons of ambition that was never the problem, it was how I focused and used it that was my problem. I was so chaotic and unorganized.

The Adderall had a way of stunting and prohibiting my growth on all spectrums of the scale. If you feel as if you can no longer think for yourself, then how are you to plan a future with goals and dreams? You can't without a vision. It all starts with a vision, and the Adderall took away that vision, and blinded me to the fact that I ever wanted to have a vision in the first place. Very scary stuff thinking back.

As a child a vision is in part all we have to build off of while trudging forward on our individual journeys. With my lack of vison, soon came my lack of imagination. When taking those pills anything and everything creative I possessed inside of me was blurred away and covered up by the medication.

I had to ask myself a simple question when I was deciding to get off the medication. It was, did I want to continue my life as a mere shell of what I truly am, roaming around lost with no real purpose or vision other than to simply *behave,* or did I want to quit the pills right now and face whatever consequences followed, in order to head down the path my true self was meant to take.

My answer to that question was instantaneous; I did not even have to think twice about it. I would rather stop medicating immediately so I could get my dreams and goals back and start living my life again, then watch my own self wither away to a state of self-pity and resentment. Making the final decision to put down the medication for good may have been one of the most important choices I have ever made so far in my life, that and quitting cigarettes.

The positive impact it has made down the road in my life is amazing. It is scary that the long term side effects are largely still unknown, I was prescribed the Adderall with complete disregard to what its effects have on me 10-20 years down the road. The only thing I regret is the fact I did not stop taking the Adderall sooner. My body, mind and soul would have thanked me in advance. But as I stated earlier it had to take what it had to take in order for me to arrive on this journey. So in conclusion I would have to say I do not regret getting off of it sooner, just extremely grateful I did find a way to stop taking the Adderall. Some people may never come to that conclusion and continue to live a soul numbing existence until the day that they die. It changed my life, that decision.

➤ CHAPTER 9

My upward journey towards growth and success once off the medication did not happen right away, matter of fact the opposite had to happen first. I had to journey down close to the bottom before I could be catapulted upwards on my journey. It always seems like it must get dark before we can experience the light.

The years after I quit taking the medication were filled with bad choices that seemed to bring me closer and closer to the bottom. It was to take me close to six years of consistent bad decision making and choices for me to finally regain control of my unmedicated behavior and impulses that ran rampant and free since the day I quit the Adderall.

It was an excruciating and painful journey I caused myself on my downward path. The simple truths I learned along the way about myself and the life around me, to this day I still consider priceless. Towards the end of high school and once I graduated (barley) high school, was when my self-medication with drinking grew quite exponentially as time progressed. I soon discovered I wasn't even making it through a full 24 hours without drinking some form of alcohol. Do I regret subjecting myself to years of personal torture and anguish? No, not exactly, if it wasn't for those years and experiences I may very well have never written this book, which would be quite a shame, seeing how this book has provided me with a healthy release of emotion and a calming effect upon my soul, but especially important, a connection to the reader. For that I am forever grateful, for all my past encounters as well as experiences, good or bad.

Once out of high school it seemed as if I attached to myself, the identity that alcohol provided me. Towards the last year of high school, it would be normal for me to drink with my friends 4-6 days of the week if not all 7 days if I could get away with it. It soon accompanied me with every single activity I would partake in, especially while hanging out with the neighborhood friends.

But once I had graduated high school, that summer I moved out of my parents' house for the very first time. In the back of my lonely mind there was a part of me that was very excited for all the drinking and partying time living on my own would produce. Even then my vision of my future was highly limited as well as quite narrow-minded and still extremely detrimental. As usual with myself and past, I always seemed to learn lessons (at least back then) the hard way. Most likely due to the fact the *lessons* tended to stick a bit better that way with me.

Once out of the house and into my apartment, which I was sharing with a co-worker, my drinking and smoking increased to daily rituals. All I ever seemed to want to do or focus on was drinking with friends. It was shortly after the time I had moved in I decided to give the local community college a go. I did not even have all the necessary pre requisites from high school, so upon my entry I was taking high school level classes to *catch* up on material so I would do ok with the other classes. I must have only done one semester, after deciding to quit and continue on without college (poor choice on my part). I did not even end with an "A" in the entry level high school pre requisite classes I was taking. I did not deserve one either.

I was 19-20 years old at the time, and I had recently been able to become a local at the neighborhood bar somehow. (Probably due to my egotistical tipping habits I provided in the beginning) The two classes I was taking at the community college were in the evenings. Usually before I would head to my evening classes I would quite often stop in at my local bar and have 2-3 *stiff* cocktails, then smoke, and head to class. Such a waste of my time and money unfortunately. As I stated previously, I did not even deserve an "A" even if they gave me one. (Which I can assure you they did not).

That was the beginning of me discovering one of my truths I was being lead to discover about myself and others, which is that honesty triumphs over all, and sooner or later it will be unavoidable. I was lying to myself while taking those classes. If I had just been completely honest with myself, and willing to ask myself some simple questions and seek the answers, then I would have saved myself a substantial amount of time and money. But as I also mentioned earlier, I tend to learn them the hard way, the lessons that is.

Once I partially got a grip on reality and willing to see the truth, I was allowed to become honest within myself and decided not to go back for the second semester. Sad, yes I know, but at least I was able to see the faults within myself and come to terms with it. After leaving my short stint of community college, I had no other vision for myself other than drinking at the neighborhood bar (underage for at least 1 year) and selling small amounts of cannabis to my friends. I had plenty of time to drink and not think about my future at all.

During that period of time my drinking and partying continued to get a bit excessive and out of hand. Of course I didn't once stop to think about what was really going on and why I was doing the things I was doing. That would have been too informative and stressful and productive for me to acknowledge and face.

So instead of focusing on my own behavior again I focused of the drugs and alcohol for quite some time. Spending so much of my time inside the bar eventually led me to some negative consequences, outside within the real world. After spending a couple hours inside drinking as usual during a lazy afternoon, I had decided I was going to finish my cocktail and head out over towards my friend's house to meet up and probably continue to drink some more. Unfortunately that never ended up happening, as I was leaving the area and getting onto the freeway, I was pulled over for speeding 5 miles over the speed limit then given a DUI. Although in my defense I was not over the lega limit whatsoever. I should have fought the case instead of settling for anything less than the truth, but I did and suffered the consequences because of the fact. But that is irrelevant now I suppose.

At the ripe age of 22 I had received my first DUI. It truly had a devastating impact upon me. Just like many people in my position, I was sure it would never be me. I was *too smart* to get one, well, we all know how that played out for me. That event brought forward to me, the notion that if I were to try and control my impulsive behavior even just a bit, then I may very well be able to avoid future situations like the one I had found myself in.

After receiving the DUI I came to the realization that I may in fact have a bit of a drinking issue. As part of my punishment with the courts, I was ordered to forego 20 Alcoholic Anonymous classes on my own accord. This is when I started to see things come around full circle. As I mentioned earlier due to quitting school after a semester, how I discovered that I needed to be honest with myself in order to grow and move forward. I was surprised to have a brief run in with that truth once attending a few AA classes as well.

I remember walking into a meeting and sitting down and reading in one of the books, how important it is for a member to be true to oneself. Matter of fact the group states it as *to thyne own self be true,* upon hearing that phrase I reflected back to almost a year prior to when I had come across and had discovered that truth already within myself. Once I realized that the group was also telling individuals the same truth more or less, I came to the realization that once again I was aligned on the correct path in my journey, being led by simple truths along the way. I never ended up staying with the group on a continual basis but I have carried with me and applied the lessons learned over the years.

It's quite humorous to me to reflect back on my experiences and seeing how all along those truths were right in front of me, I just was not tuned into the right vision to allow myself to see it. I once again seemed to have to discover it the *hard* way as previously stated with all my prior life lessons and truths. That is just the way it has been with myself up until now. Did it always have to be that way? Looking back, no probably not, but I would not have found the answers any other way. The past events had to unfold accordingly for me to be writing to you, the reader.

Another powerful truth I came across that once learned, accepted and applied, helped pull me away from my downward dip, was realizing that in order to get from point A to point B I must become willing to do the necessary disciplines to sacrifice who I am for who I can become. That was a very profound truth for me to come across, even more so once it got applied to my life. In order to counteract the force that was pulling me downward I needed something just as powerful pulling me in the opposite direction. That was the beginning of my *why* that propelled me forward on my journey. So many times I neglected myself of that question, the question of who could I become. I had a limited mindset of myself and my future and once I accepted that truth only then did things start to change.

In order for me to not only except but apply that truth, I had to let go of still more identities that I allowed my friends, family and authoritarian figures to place upon me. I was still off the medication, yet demonstrated the exact same ability to allow the opinions and notions of others to actually affect me and bother me enough to begin to attach myself to that vision they had of me or my behavior. It fixed the short term problem of disruptiveness but had long term consequences and side effects for myself.

One of those things that I had to slowly chip away at and on, was my ego, which encouraged boisterous habitual drinking in order for me to feel superior in some strange way, or so I thought. I had to first even realize I had an ego that is how bad my ego was. Once realizing it was there within me affecting every part of my life, I was then able to accept it for what it was and move on to the process of trying to diminish it, which I did a horrible job at but at least it left me to the point that I came to the conclusion that if I wanted a change I had to be willing to sacrifice who I was for what I could become. I am grateful for those experiences and insights.

After the DUI my drinking continued excessively for about another few months or so. It was at that point I decided I would have enough, and quit drinking for nearly 2 years altogether. It did not last though; unfortunately I allowed the stress of work and life's daily absurdities to break me and threw in the towel at the 2 year mark. That brief period was a rough one for me, instead of seeing it for what it truly was, I threw my hands up and just accepted I had to drink and that is the way it is. Thankfully nothing last forever, not even that mentality of mine. Once out of my personal storm I was able to re-focus myself and start to create a vision of my future for the first time in my life.

➢ CHAPTER 10

The beginning of my un-medicated journey to a successful (in my opinion) and purposeful life, I would say had to start with my concept and identity of time, having to grow and expand upon it, and that could not have possibly happened if my earlier path and experiences leading me to a bit of self-awareness never occurred. So you see it all had to take place in the correct order in which it did for everything to *line up*. Stressing out over ones past is always a waste of time becasue we needed that past to determine and project our own futures. Once my mind had cleared up from the Adderall, then years later the alcohol and drug use, I was able to see time for what it truly was, highly precious and extremely valuable.

My limited vision of time transcended into a limited vision of my future; they go hand in hand. I had to change my whole philosophy of what time and my life meant to me, and how I would go about using it and applying it practically, and efficiently. Before I did not utilize my time wisely up to this point whatsoever. I would stay up extremely late and sleep half the day away, it was impossible to maintain productivity with such a casual schedule. No matter what was happening in my life or around me I could never utilize my time in a manner at which it would bring me one step closer to my goals and success, most likely because I had no such goals or visions around the beginning of that time period.

Once I realized how much I was truly wasting time, my goals and visions all blossomed into plans and ideas. That was the beginning journey towards success and action for me. Once my vision of time matured I started to plan accordingly. I was able to break down and focus on what I needed to accomplish first and what needed to become prioritized throughout my day in order to maximize my own efficiency.

I was beginning to finally learn how to manage my impulsiveness and use my creative energy towards more positive elements in my life. Up until this point if you were to mention success to me I would have thought it just came along to the lucky or more fortunate few. It never occurred to me that you had to plan for success or that it was also predictable based upon what you do on a daily basis. It was the mindset of an ill-informed, ignorant child. By any means how would I ever stumble upon success randomly while doing nothing to prepare, it was nonsense, but that was my philosophy early on in life.

Once I committed to focusing my attention onto constructive things, it then opened the door for me to take the idea of finding a fulfilling successful life and put it into action, well at least in the beginning make a fulltime attempt towards something somewhat good instead of wasting away in a journal of unused ideas and a puddle of stale beer. I had to at all costs keep progressing and moving forward in order for me to stay committed to my vision of success at all times. In the early stages of my journey I did not take the idea of success that seriously at all, I was just aware that if I talked about it and pointed myself in that vague direction, that hopefully things would start to change ever so slowly. Eventually they did, but very small almost unnoticeable changes, almost as if I could *feel* the change before anyone could *see* the changes. Things are not always as chaotic as they appear to be when you go back and replay your own time line of events. They say when you are in the middle of growth and change that it may very well feel painful and confusing, not like growth, but that is how you know growth is occurring.

Once my intent was set daily on discovering success, truths and concepts started unveiling themselves to me as time went on. I soon realized if I was to use my energy and impulse for good in my life then I needed to focus it on life's daily disciplines. At the time I had yet to discover self-freedom through self-discipline. My unfocused impulses always convinced me to just do whatever I wanted whenever I wanted, regardless of the consequences, but that is not how you arrive towards success.

I had to start with the idea that everything I did mattered. Let me explain, I could not begin to develop an attention to detail if I never started paying attention to the inner things to begin with. Everything mattered, every choice and decision mattered, and I mattered. As soon as I had begun to apply that new philosophy to my life, I started to be able to recognize and notice all the chaos in and around my life. By continuing the day with the idea that everything I did mattered, it allowed me to not only be aware of the chaos but finally able to work on it and organize and get rid of some of it all. That was an extremely freeing truth to experience and come across. Potentially very well could have changed my life, who knows. By applying and executing that philosophy I was able to start seeing the importance and value in what I did and accomplished each waking day.

I was finally able to let go of other people's identity of me and focus on who I truly was meant to become, which I feel is a vessel of truth and to communicate that in the written word form by any means necessary for the people. If we do not have truth then can we have anything at all? Because anything else would just be a lie in that sense. Everyone wants to find meaning and purpose in their lives, but not everyone is willing to put in the work to find out those answers, because it is quite possible to live your life with no goals or purpose and merely exist like a ghost floating through the empty void of space. What a horrible way to spend your life if you ask me. That is why I became so dedicated in my pursuit. I had to become relentless with my disciplines and actions.

As someone much smarter than me once stated "the pursuit of goals is what gives life its sustaining meaning." as long as I remained focused and productive, the good news was that I most certainly would continue to grow. As I continued to no longer neglect my small daily disciplines, I soon started to notice not only the quality of my overall life start to improve piece by piece, but my self-confidence slowly started to build back up as well, which was quite refreshing to say the least.

I felt like I needed to continually build on what I had previously learned the day prior or else my momentum would be slow down or lost completely. The last daily discipline that I had originally started, along with those others was to be thankful every day. Now by no means was that or still is an easy task for me, it is something I need to practice daily without fail. By being thankful for life's daily occurrences I started to become aware of the fact that there are people who would kill to be in my shoes even on my worst day. In order to practice gratitude, my perspective along the way had to mature and morph, it was the only way I could then be truly appreciative of what I was going through and where I was supposed to be going, and the only way my perspective was to ever mature was by practicing the disciplines every day starting as soon as I woke up each morning. Even when I felt like nothing was working and felt like giving up and resorting back to my old impulsive behavior, I stuck to my plan and continued to move forward each and every day. Always remember that when things go wrong, don't go with them!

It was extremely important for me to stay as self-aware as possible during this period of growth and transformation. If I were to let my guard down for even a day my progress would be restarted and potentially lost all together. That could have had disastrous affects on me, because who knows, it could have leaded me to going back on the medication. Thank god that never happened and I did continue to grow in the other direction. Life is truly all about experiences and the intensity at which you feel those experiences. Being able to be off the Adderall for a lengthy amount of time and working on myself to move towards success, allowed me to feel that bright intensity of life again and allowed me to create even more memorable experiences than I had previously had while on the Adderall. I was able to accumulate and continually add to the intensity that I felt during my experiences. It had allowed me to zero in and try to discover purpose within my life.

It was through the creation of experiences that allowed me to find my purpose, and through the act of daily disciplines, allowed me to grow my purpose, refine and try to master it, and then share it to all by giving away what freely came to me. That is how we can make today a bit better than the day before and how can we help others by working on eliminating one another's suffering, even if it is only for a moment or two. The important thing is that we share our success (and failures) with one another to help lift each other up in times of need and desperation. Nobody can do this thing called *life* alone, whether you like that idea or not, we truly need one another, as much as we tend to like to think otherwise.

Often times on the journey towards success (myself included) we are apprehensive to share and discuss our failures, quite possibly out of fear of being rejected or looked upon as not good enough. I am here to tell the reader that it is impossible to succeed without experiencing tons of failure. Failure must be embraced and tolerated.

As soon as I came to my own conclusion that I had to embrace failure at all costs if I wanted to achieve a successful, meaningful life, I then realized that I only get what I deserve, not what I want, and in order to try and get what I deserved meant that I had to try and fail and keep trying every single day I opened my eyes. My pursuit had to be relentless in the face of adversity and setbacks. This is how when channeled properly, my ADHD seemed to finally work in my advantage and favor for once.

Once I had accepted and in a way embraced my own failures, my fear soon seemed to dim down each passing day. With that new found acceptance of failure I discovered that my personal goals and dreams seemed to be growing in the coming months. The path was leaving me more and more hungry for truth, knowledge, and personal development, than seemingly every before.

I was finally becoming willing to sacrifice who I was in order to become who I was always meant to be. I want the reader to understand that if I could learn how to focus and control my energy and mind for the greater good and come across these truths, then immediately put them into action, that they too can find success in these behavioral patterns but do not forget you must act upon it immediately and start small but be consistent and never let up in your pursuit. I always had to remind myself along the way that success is something you attract by what you become, that was very powerful for me to remember that at all times.

➢ CHAPTER 11

All of which I had experienced and learned leading up to the current time in my life has been put through the test of time over and over again and has always came out on the other side unscathed. That is only true due to the fact that they were honest truths and the truth never fades, it will remain standing in the face of destruction and ashes, may not be immediately recognizable but eventually it will re appear, standing tall and bold.

As of currently, it has been 12 years since I last was prescribed Adderall, and 20 years since I was first diagnosed, a lot has occurred within that time frame in my life. It has not always been a beautiful path leading me thus far, but I suppose there is always beauty to be found in the flaws and imperfections of life.

I have been able to apply my new philosophies and truths to my daily life for over 3 years now and things have been far more productive and fulfilling than ever before in my past. To this day I still continue to practice and not neglect life's daily disciplines. That is how I manage to get the most out of each day yet be able to have the flexibility to adapt when changes occur, which they will, that is most certain. Matter of fact the only thing guaranteed in this life is change.

Part of my current growth I have received stems from my daily disciplines continually evolving. I now have been able to wake up at four in the morning seven days a week now for the last 3 months. That may not seem like growth to everyone but I am now able to accomplish much more throughout my day by allowing myself a bit more time throughout my day. I would not have been able to keep my progression evolving if it was not for focusing on the daily disciplines. Working on disciplines daily brought about a level of patience and grit I have never been able to experience before. It has been a long way coming from sleeping in until 10:30-11:00am to consistently rising at 4am and then attacking my morning with strength, vigor and determination. I want everyone to know that it is possible to retrain your mind and carve out a new road for oneself, it just may take a lot of failures, detours and rerouting to find what best works for you, it is possible, I am here to tell you that it truly is.

I cannot reiterate how important goal setting was and still is to me and my life. Setting and striving towards meeting my own personal goals has helped developed and change me in ways I never thought possible. Upon awakening at my standard 4am wakeup time I immediately sit down at my desk and first give thanks and express gratitude for all that is in my life. We must remember to not forget to notice the small daily beautiful things that occur every day in our lives. Beauty is all around us we just need to expand our vision to be able to capture bits of it.

I then continue every morning to plan out how I want my day to go. I plan it as if I was planning/scheduling my perfect day more or less. By putting it down on paper it now holds me accountable for what I do or do not end up accomplishing by the end of the 24 hour period. It took me 26 years of living and learning to finally make plans and a list, then execute on them. Just imagine where I would be now if I started 10 years ago. My vision of the future seemed to expand as I continued my expansion of goal setting. At first my goals were only small daily goals, now I still have those as well, but now I also incorporate my long term goals, the ones that seem crazy to others. To be able to see where you want to be in 5, 6, or 10 years is a valuable asset. It took me quite some time to learn how to properly set and work towards achieving my goals. It was well worth the wait and work to learn such a life changing technique.

I had to start out small, very small. In the beginning, I had to just set 1 or 2 small daily goals that I knew I could accomplish if I followed through with each one of them. Once I was able to consistently accomplish the 1 or 2 small goals, only then did I start to dig a bit deeper. The important part for me was the consistency part. If I could manage to accomplish 2 goals every day, I just thought to myself what more could I possibly do in a 24 hour period if I expanded my vision towards my goals. From that point on my list kept growing. Now it is so automatic for me half the time I find myself not writing them down on paper, instead organizing them in my head, I am not condoning or encouraging that, it's just for me, it is so engrained into me that it is a part of me now. I try to execute to the best of my abilities every single day.

I cannot reiterate how important it is to maintain consistency on the journey towards success. I cannot even count how many times I would say I was going to do something, then either do it for only a few times or not do anything at all. Without consistency in my life my growth was extremely limited and stunted. I now strive to be consistent within every aspect of my life. I'm far from achieving 100% but it is always on my mind every single day I need to make a tough decision. I remember to stay consistent in my healthy choices and routines. I promise that if you stay consistent in your productive ways not only will you grow but your self-confidence will begin to rise as well, and in doing so the consistency will eventually become part of your daily routine and it will become embedded in your mind, it will become a healthy habit. It took me too long to develop and maintain healthy habits of my own. It was not until I was able to master my daily disciplines that I began to notice more and more healthy habits being integrated into my own personal life.

It goes back to what I stated earlier, that everything we do matters. Everything we do either brings us one step closer to a successful life or one step further away from a successful life. Everything I have learned and experienced leading up to this point in my life had been a building block towards success. Each new day I would build on what I had previously learned the day prior. At first it was small painful baby steps with lots of confusion and failure thrown into the mix, but as I practice and apply my tools and resources presented to me, I have come to see the path and steps get a bit clearer as I trudge forward to become who I was always meant to become.

Everyone has a purpose in this life, my hope for you is that something you read throughout this book will very possibly provide you that spark needed for you to realize what it is and who you truly are meant to be, and when you do find it, you apply some of the principles and lessons I had to learn along the way to help give light and energy to your purpose and passion. We must continue to strive for growth and continue to execute, then communicate and share our experiences with one another, for the sole purpose of lifting each other up and continuing the flow of knowledge and ideas. Ideas can be extremely life changing. Once I had a vision, my ideas seemed to grow rapidly and consistently. If we do not pass on what we learn and know, then how possibly can we expect to make any positive change in the world without causing more harm then we previously had in the past? It is due to the fact that we pass on and share what we have learned with others, that helps continue the cycle of growth and passion.

None of this was fast development for me; it was an excruciating slow, at times painful journey. We must understand that anything worth having in this lifetime will at times feel slow and painful while striving toward it as well. I can promise you that on the other side of pain is something magnificent and extraordinary, you must keep moving forward by any means necessary. I am willing to do today what others don't do in order to get tomorrow what others won't get. It is due to all these small life changes that I started to act upon daily, that my life has been successful so far. I am far from where I need to be, but want to demonstrate how far one can develope from our usual standard into someone we never imagined possible. It is extraordinary to witness that type of transformation, not only within myself but within others as well. It makes it all worth it to bear witness to such positive changes.

That brings me to something I recently have come to terms with and started to understand and grasp, and that is the statement that success is something you attract only by what you have become. My current self is now ready and willing to do whatever it takes on a daily basis to get one step closer to attracting success. When I talk about my life becoming successful I need the reader to know that I am not talking about personal finances or materialistic objects, I am simply referring to my individual goals and how I live out my life's purpose and meaning, then be able to share it and communicate it with others in order to create some sort of lasting positive change or connection. We must never forget that we all are truly connected to one another down to our eternal core and consciousness.

Obtaining *things* has never been an honest desire of mine; I respect the journey too much to define it with a numerical number, which in return merits a certain level of success. To me it is endless; the potential for knowledge and growth then the ability to share and spread it is endless and amazing. If you would have asked my past self-years ago if I was to write a book, I would have looked at you as if you were crazy. I probably would have said something along the lines of "do I look like I could write a book?" and laugh or shrug, then walk away. So foolish and so limited of my thinking to set such ridiculous restrictions upon myself before even trying. I was self-sabotaging myself and I was not even aware of the fact at the time. It truly is amazing what a bit of self-awareness can provide for your future, when even applying just a little bit at first. That is all it takes to get the wheels moving at times. It quite often leads to the pursuit of knowledge because then that knowledge turns into growth, which in return we then are able to truly see what we are honestly capable of and are then motivated to build toward that on a daily basis.

It has been very nice to be able to look back on the last couple years of my life with absolutely no regrets or contempt, because I know every day is a chance to improve and grow from the last. In order for me to experience a breakthrough in growth I had to become ready to be able to master my own breaking point. What I mean by that is that I had to be willing to try to master myself when everything was going wrong and all my life seemed to produce was low moments and chaos. When I got to the point of wanting to give up and throw the towel in that is when I decided I must master my breaking point or it will break and absolutely destroy me. That is when I decided that I will no longer be a victim in this life and that I will continue to push forward with growth and change by any means necessary. I finally learned how to convert my pain into strength and determination.

We are far from perfect, and so is this world that we live in, but that does not mean we cannot strive each and every day to become a better version of ourselves each day and in the process make the world a bit better than it was the day before. Nothing worth having in this life will ever come easy to you, that I can promise. You will fail and fail again. That part is not what is important. The important part is that you master your breaking point and keep trying and executing until something positive comes from it, and if something positive never comes from it, well then you learned what not to do within the failures. It is a win win when it comes to knowledge and growth. I truly wish you all the best in your journey towards success. Never settle for less, take advice, not orders and always make sure that what you do is a product of your own conclusion. Take good notes and always stay well prepared. If I could turn my life of lost potential into something great, and quit the medication after a decade of use, then grow and strive for my own personal success against all odds, than you must understand that you too can accomplish and achieve whatever you truly want to do. Always remember to protect and nourish your mind at all costs and once you learn what you are supposed to learn, and achieve what you are supposed to achieve, always remember to pass it along and share with others in order to continually teach and help lift one another up. This life is too short to remain absent minded of others. We must give back in order to receive. Always remember you get what you deserve, not what you want. My beautiful sweet daughter, please always remember that you are the embodiment of limitless human potential and love. You are capable of achieving absolutely anything, and when things go wrong (which they undoubtedly will) stay centered and true to yourself, and remind yourself of one simple thing, when things go wrong do not go with them. Keep your head up and back straight and continue to make your own path in life. I only wish the best for each and every one of you.

> ## CHAPTER 12

Life, obviously, can be a wild ride at times. The sole fact that I made it to this point in my life, able to write a book and be able to connect with readers all around the world, still truly amazes me. All I ever wanted was to be able to thrive in what I was passionate about and continually strive to become better than I was the day before.

I am grateful and humbled to share my story with you all. If even a single reader of this book takes something from it and critically applies it to his or her life, I feel I will have done my job as a writer – and will be forever thankful that you found truth within these pages. I can't stress enough how important books are to my life; it's as if every book I read turns out, somehow, to be the perfect sequel to the last, the perfect successor in the long, winding stream of literature trailing behind me, stretching out before me all at once. The flow of continual knowledge is amazing when you just keep reading to the best of your own ability. Thanks to lots of practice, I can now read, with a fair degree of proficiency and comprehension, an average of four novel-length books per month. That is huge progress for someone who, not even a year earlier, was scarcely able to read even one such book in the same span (and actually understand most of what he was reading, that is).

Most of the time, I do not even need to search for my next book to read; I usually just stay quiet and listen to things and people around me. Nine times out of ten, I will hear about or come across books I have never even heard of before; usually, I'll find that I want to investigate them further, if not actually end up reading them. As a kid in elementary school, I was quite obsessed with reading. For a while I was reading any and every chance I got. I think I loved the escape it provided me at the time; it just always felt so *right* to me.

As my passion for books and reading grew and developed further, so did my passion and interest for writing. I rather loathed the actual classroom environment itself, especially the whole "sitting and listening to the teacher" part, but I always loved reading and writing. I suppose it was because I could get lost within myself and get creative, instead of sitting at a table and be indoctrinated by some teacher who does not even really care to perceive what is really going on at that moment in time. For most it was quite obvious that it was just a paycheck to them, and the few who taught for the love of knowledge and teaching itself stood out in my memory as clear as day still.

Writing almost became sacred in a way to me, it was a place I could go to and communicate, even if it was to just myself. It always made me feel sharper and more improved as an individual. As I grew older, I found myself straying further and further away from writing as time went on. It soon got to the point where I stopped reading and writing altogether, though I'm not sure exactly why. Quite possibly out of fear of what others may have thought about me, I'm not quite sure why.

During my elementary school days, I found myself obsessed with poetry, I even constructed my own binder and compiled all my most recent poems inside of it. I would just sit and write poems all day long, I recall as a young child going to what our school called the "Young Authors' Conference." It was for students who showed an interest and passion for writing. I recall getting picked to go two years in a row for my class, and both years that I attended I brought my book of poems with me to share, well to be exact, the second time I attended I had written a short novel to go with my book of poems.

I remember feeling very free and whole whenever I wrote. It was the one thing someone with authority could not take from me or tell me how to do it. My ambition towards writing came from a deep source within my soul it felt like, it felt so good to be a part of something much bigger than myself for once. In my world of chaos my words offered me a balance that I so desperately needed.

Who knows where I would be now if I had continued to read and write and develop my skills over the 6 years that I quit reading and writing, what a shame. During that time period I did absolutely no reading and writing, and instead filled my days and mind with things that had absolutely zero positive impact upon myself and others. That time period was filled with wasted potential and ability, it seemed as if I had lost sight of who I was and allowed my vision of myself to become extremely distorted and toxic.

Don't ever stop doing the things that you love and that make you happy, strictly out of fear of what others may think and say of you. I am telling you right now that it is not worth damaging or losing your soul over. This life is way too short to be anything but the best version of yourself that you can possibly be at all times. It will not be easy to follow your correct path, but I can guarantee you that it will be well worth it for you and your mind. You can tell what is and what isn't important to you by the simple fact that no matter how long you seem to go without doing the thing you love to do, you will always come back to thinking about it. There is simply no escaping from it; if you were meant to create, then – if you're anything like me, anyway – you must create by any means necessary, or else suffer the consequences (in short, a feeling of restlessness and irritability, of being spiritually stymied and emotionally unfulfilled, as if your time on earth were essentially squandered).

For myself, the choice is really quite simple, is really no choice at all: either I continually create new things, art of some form or another (be it writing, painting, doodling, or whatever), or else my soul rapdily withers, eventually to perish in agony. I have tried in the past to stop creating and to just numb myself instead; it has never worked; I have always come back, sooner or later, to the act of creating (and the sooner I did, the better off I was for it). It's in my DNA, I think, or had might as well be. Any time I'm so foolish or lazy as to cease creating, invariably I find myself riddled with anxiety, or plagued by depression. The point is, the result is never pretty.

The process of creation, in sum, and seemingly *only* that process, affords me the constructive outlet I require to express my thoughts and feelings – in other words, to express *myself* – in a fashion that is at once responsible and supremely satisfying. It is only through the act of creating that I am truly able to live in the now, to meditate on what it means to be alive in this time and place, and to be at peace with it at all: with myself, with my past, with the world, with all my darkest memories and bleakest hours and fondest hopes and most precious, secret dreams. You know the kind I mean: the ones we hardly dare to dream at all, but must, that we might find the will, somehow, to face another day – and another, and yet one more.

Thank you for reading my book. May you find purpose in all that you do.

13791064R00061

Made in the USA
San Bernardino, CA
22 December 2018